PLATO and a PLATYPUS WALK into a BAR...

PLATO and a PLATYPUS WALK into a BAR ...

Understanding Philosophy Through Jokes

Daniel Klein

Thomas Cathcart

ONEWORLD

A Oneworld Book

Published in Great Britain and Australia
by Oneworld Publications, 2016

First published in the English language in 2006
by Harry N. Abrams, Incorporated, New York

ISBN 978-1-78607-018-0
eISBN 978-1-78607-019-7

Printed and bound in Great Britain by Clays Ltd, St Ives plc

Oneworld Publications
10 Bloomsbury Street
London WC1B 3SR
England

To the memory of our philosophical grandfather

GROUCHO MARX,

who summed up our basic ideology when he said,

"These are my principles; if you don't like them, I have others."

CONTENTS

Philogagging

An Introduction

DIMITRI: If Atlas holds up the world, what holds up Atlas?

TASSO: Atlas stands on the back of a turtle.

DIMITRI: But what does the turtle stand on?

TASSO: Another turtle.

DIMITRI: And what does *that* turtle stand on?

TASSO: My dear Dimitri, *it's turtles all the way down!*

This bit of ancient Greek dialogue perfectly illustrates the philosophical notion of infinite regress, a concept that comes up when we ask if there is a First Cause—of life, of the universe, of time and space, and most significantly, of a Creator. Something must have created the Creator, so the causal buck—or turtle—cannot stop with him. Or with the Creator behind him. Or the one behind him. It's Creators all the way down—or up, if that seems like the right direction for chasing down Creators.

If you find that infinite regress is getting you nowhere fast, you might consider the doctrine of *creatio ex nihilo*—creation out of nothing—or, as John Lennon put it in a slightly different context, "Before Elvis, there was nothing."

But let's lend an ear to old Tasso again. As well as being illuminating, his rejoinder—"It's turtles all the way down!"—definitely has the ring of a punch line. *Ba-da-bing!*

That's no surprise to us. The construction and payoff of jokes and the construction and payoff of philosophical concepts are made out of the same stuff. They tease the mind in similar ways. That's because philosophy and jokes proceed from the same impulse: to confound our sense of the way things are, to flip our worlds upside down, and to ferret out hidden, often uncomfortable, truths about life. What the philosopher calls an insight, the gagster calls a zinger.

For example, consider the following classic joke. On the surface, it just sounds deliciously goofy, but on closer inspection it speaks to the very heart of British empiricist philosophy—the question of what sort of information about the world we can depend on.

Morty comes home to find his wife and his best friend, Lou, naked together in bed. Just as Morty is about to open his mouth,

Lou jumps out of the bed and says, "Before you say anything, old pal, what are you going to believe, me or your eyes?"

By challenging the primacy of sensory experience, Lou raises the question of what sort of data is certain and why. Is one way of gathering facts about the world—say, *seeing*—more dependable than others—say, a leap of faith that accepts Lou's description of reality?

Here's another example of a philogag, this one a riff on the Argument from Analogy, which says that if two outcomes are similar, they must have a similar cause:

A ninety-year-old man went to the doctor and said, "Doctor, my eighteen-year-old wife is expecting a baby."

The doctor said, "Let me tell you a story. A man went hunting, but instead of a gun, he picked up an umbrella by mistake. When a bear suddenly charged at the man, he picked up the umbrella, shot the bear, and killed it."

The man said, "Impossible. Someone else must have shot that bear."

The doctor said, "My point exactly!"

You couldn't ask for a better illustration of the Argument from Analogy, a philosophical ploy currently (and erroneously) being used in the argument for Intelligent Design (i.e., if there's an eyeball, there must be an Eyeball-Designer-in-the-Sky.)

We could go on and on—and in fact we will, from Agnosticism to Zen, from Hermeneutics to Eternity. We will show how philosophical concepts can be illuminated by jokes *and* how many jokes are loaded with fascinating philosophical content. Wait a second, are those two notions the same? Can we get back to you on that?

STUDENTS wandering into a philosophy class are usually hoping to gain some perspective on, say, the meaning of it all, but then some rumpled guy in mismatched tweeds ambles up to the podium and starts lecturing on the meaning of "meaning."

First things first, he says. Before we answer any question, big or small, we need to understand what the question itself signifies. Listening reluctantly, we soon discover that what this guy has to say is wicked interesting.

That's just the way philosophy—and philosophers—are. Questions beget questions, and those questions beget another whole generation of questions. *It's questions all the way down.*

We may start with basic ones like, "What is the meaning of it all?" and, "Does God exist?" and, "How can I be true to myself?" and, "Am I in the wrong classroom?" but very quickly we discover we need to ask other questions in order to answer our original questions. This process has given rise to an array of philosophical disciplines, each delving into particular Big Questions by asking and attempting to answer the questions that underlie them. Any questions?

So it follows that, "What is the meaning of it all?" is dealt with in the discipline known as Metaphysics, and "Does God exist?" in the one called, Philosophy of Religion. "How can I be true to myself?" falls to the school of Existentialism; "Am I in the wrong classroom?" to the new sector of philosophy called Meta-philosophy, which poses the question, "What is philosophy?" And on it goes, with each sphere of philosophy undertaking different kinds of questions and concepts.

We've arranged this book not chronologically, but by those questions we had in mind when we wandered into that first philosophy classroom—and the philosophical disciplines that tackle them. What's so neat is that a whole bunch of jokes just happen to occupy the identical conceptual territory as these disciplines. (Pure chance? Or is there an Intelligent Designer after all?) And there is a big reason why this is all so neat: When the two of us wandered *out* of that classroom, we were so baffled and bewildered, we were convinced we'd never get our minds around this heady stuff. That's when a graduate student sauntered up to us and told us the joke about Morty coming home to find his best friend, Lou, in bed with his wife.

"Now *that's* philosophy!" he said.

We call it philogagging.

THOMAS CATHCART
DANIEL KLEIN

Metaphysics

Metaphysics tackles the Big Questions head on:
What is being? What is the nature of reality? Do we have
free will? How many angels can dance on the head of a pin?
How many does it take to change a lightbulb?

DIMITRI: Something's been bothering me lately, Tasso.

TASSO: What's that?

DIMITRI: What is the meaning of it all?

TASSO: All what?

DIMITRI: You know, life, death, love—the whole stuffed grape leaf.

TASSO: What makes you think any of it has any meaning?

DIMITRI: Because it has to. Otherwise life would just be…

TASSO: What?

DIMITRI: I need an ouzo.

Teleology

Does the universe have a purpose?

According to Aristotle, *everything* has a *telos,* which is an inner goal it is meant to attain. An acorn has a telos: an oak tree. It's what an acorn is "meant to be." Birds have one; bees have one. They say that down in Boston even beans have one. It's part of the very structure of reality.

If that seems a little abstract, in the following story Mrs. Goldstein telescopes the *telos* down to earth.

Mrs. Goldstein was walking down the street with her two grandchildren. A friend stopped to ask her how old they were.
She replied, "The doctor is five and the lawyer is seven."

Does human life have a *telos?*

Aristotle thought so. He thought the *telos* of human life is happiness, a point disputed by other philosophers throughout human history. St. Augustine, seven centuries later, thought the *telos* of life is to love God. To a twentieth-century existentialist like Martin Heidegger, man's *telos* is to live without denial of the true human condition, particularly death. *Happiness? How shallow!*

Meaning-of-life jokes have multiplied as fast as meanings of life, which in turn have multiplied as fast as philosophers.

A seeker has heard that the wisest guru in all of India lives atop India's highest mountain. So the seeker treks over hill and Delhi until he reaches the fabled mountain. It's incredibly steep, and more than once he slips and falls. By the time he reaches the top, he is full of cuts and bruises, but there is the guru, sitting cross-legged in front of his cave.

"O, wise guru," the seeker says, "I have come to you to ask what the secret of life is."

"Ah, yes, the secret of life," the guru says. "The secret of life is a teacup."

"A teacup? I came all the way up here to find the meaning of life, and you tell me it's a teacup!"

The guru shrugs. "So maybe it isn't a teacup."

This guru is acknowledging that formulating the *telos* of life is a slippery business. Furthermore, it's not everybody's cup of tea.

There is a distinction between the *telos* of life—what human beings are *meant* to be—and a particular individual's goals in life—what he *wants* to be. Is Sam, the dentist in the following story, really seeking the universal *telos* of life or simply doing his own thing? His mother clearly has her own idea of the *telos* of her son's life.

A young dentist called Sam went off to India to find the meaning of life. Months went by and his mother didn't hear a word from him. Finally, she took a plane to India and asked for the wisest man there. She was directed to an ashram, where the guard told her that she would have to wait a week for an audience with the guru, and at that time she would only be allowed to speak three words to him. She waited, carefully preparing her words. When she was finally ushered in to see the guru, she said to him, "Sam, come home!"

Look up "metaphysics" in the dictionary and it tells you the word stems from the title of a treatise by Aristotle and that it deals with questions at a level of abstraction beyond (*meta*) scientific observation. But this turns out to be a case of what is known in Latin as *post hoc hokum.* In fact, Aristotle didn't call his treatise "metaphysics" at all, let alone because it dealt with questions beyond the purview of science. Actually, it was given that name in the first century A.D. by an editor of Aristotle's collected works, who chose the title because that chapter was "beyond" (i.e., came after) Aristotle's treatise on "Physics."

Essentialism

What is the structure of reality? What specific attributes make things what they are? Or as philosophers are wont to say, What attributes make things not what they aren't?

Aristotle drew a distinction between *essential* and *accidental* properties. The way he put it is that essential properties are those without which a thing wouldn't be what it is, and accidental properties are those that determine *how* a thing is, but not *what* it is. For example, Aristotle thought that rationality was essential to being a human being and, since Socrates was a human being, Socrates's rationality was essential to his being Socrates. Without the property of rationality, Socrates simply wouldn't be Socrates. He wouldn't even be a human being, so how could he be Socrates? On the other hand, Aristotle thought that Socrates's property of being snub-nosed was merely accidental; snub-nosed was part of *how* Socrates was, but it wasn't essential to what or who he was. To put it another way, take away Socrates's rationality, and he's no longer Socrates, but give him plastic surgery, and he's Socrates with a nose job. Which reminds us of a joke.

When Thompson hit seventy, he decided to change his lifestyle completely so that he could live longer. He went on a strict diet, he jogged, he swam, and he went sunbathing. In just three months' time, Thompson lost thirty pounds, reduced his waist by six inches, and expanded his chest by five inches. Svelte and tanned, he decided to top it all off with a sporty new haircut. Afterward, while stepping out of the barbershop, he was hit by a bus.

As he lay dying, he cried out, "God, how could you do this to me?"

And a voice from the heavens responded, "To tell you the truth, Thompson, I didn't recognize you."

Poor Thompson seems to have changed certain accidental properties of himself, although we recognize that he is still essentially Thompson. So does Thompson for that matter. In fact, both of these conditions are essential to the joke. Ironically, the only character in the joke who does *not* recognize Thompson is God, who you'd think would be essentially omniscient.

The distinction between essential and accidental properties is illustrated by a number of other jokes in this vein.

Abe: I've got a riddle for you, Sol. What's green, hangs on the wall, and whistles?

Sol: I give up.

Abe: A herring.

Sol: But a herring isn't green.

Abe: So you can paint it green.

Sol: But a herring doesn't hang on the wall.

Abe: Put a nail through it, it hangs on the wall.

Sol: But a herring doesn't whistle!

Abe: So? It doesn't whistle.

The following version probably won't garner you many laughs at the comedy store, but it may win you a few points at the British Philosophical Association's annual meeting.

Abe: What is the object "X" that has the properties of greenness, wall-suspension, and whistling capability?

Sol: I can't think of anything that fits that description.

Abe: A herring.

Sol: A herring doesn't have greenness.

Abe: Not as an *essential* property, Solly. But a herring could be *accidentally* green, no? Try painting it. You'll see.

Sol: But a herring doesn't have wall-suspension.

Abe: But what if you accidentally nail it to the wall?

Sol: How could you accidentally nail a herring to the wall?

Abe: Trust me. Anything's possible. That's philosophy.

Sol: Okay, but a herring doesn't whistle, even accidentally.

Abe: So sue me.

Sol and Abe turn to face the B.P.A. audience, which is totally silent.

Sol: What is this, a convention of Stoics? Hey, Nietzsche got bigger laughs when he played the Vatican.

Sometimes an object has properties that at first blush seem to be accidental, but turn out to be accidental only within certain limits, as illustrated in this gag.

"Why is an elephant big, grey, and wrinkled?"
"Because if it was small, white, and round, it'd be an aspirin."

We can picture an elephant on the small side; we'd call it "a small elephant." We can even picture an elephant a sort of dusty brown; we would call it "a sort of dusty-brown elephant." And an elephant without wrinkles would be "an unwrinkled elephant." In other words, bigness, greyness, and wrinkledness all fail Aristotle's test of defining what an elephant *essentially* is. Instead they describe how elephants are, generally and *accidentally*. The joke says, though, that this is true only up to a point. Something as small, white, and round as an aspirin cannot be an elephant, and confronted with such an object, we would not be tempted to ask, "Is that an aspirin you're taking, Bob, or an atypical elephant?"

The point is that bigness, greyness, and wrinkledness are not precise enough terms to be the essential qualities of an elephant. It's a certain size *range* and a certain colour *range* that, among other qualities, determine whether or not something is an elephant. Wrinkledness, on the other hand, may be a red herring, or perhaps a whistling herring.

Rationalism

Now for something completely different—a school of metaphysics that has produced literally volumes of satire without any help from us. There's only one problem: The jokes all miss the point.

When the seventeenth-century rationalist philosopher Gottfried Wilhelm Leibniz famously said, "This is the best of all possible worlds," he opened himself to unmerciful ridicule. It all began in the following century with *Candide,* Voltaire's very funny novel of a good-natured young man (Candide) and his philosophical mentor, Dr. Pangloss (Voltaire's rendition of

Leibniz). In his journeys, young Candide encounters floggings, unjust executions, epidemics, and an earthquake patterned after the Lisbon earthquake of 1755, which had levelled the city. Nothing, however, can shake Dr. Pangloss's insistence that "Everything is for the best in this best of all possible worlds." When Candide sets out to save Jacques, a Dutch Anabaptist, from drowning, Pangloss stops him by proving that the Bay of Lisbon had been "formed expressly for the Anabaptist to drown in."

Two centuries later, Leonard Bernstein's 1956 musical, *Candide*, added to the joke. The show's best-known song, "The Best of All Possible Worlds," has Pangloss and the cast sing Richard Wilbur's lyrics praising war as a blessing in disguise, because it unites us all—as victims.

Terry Southern and Mason Hoffenberg joined the fun with their ribald version, *Candy*, about a naïve young girl, who, despite being taken advantage of by all the men she meets, remains innocent and optimistic. It was made into a 1964 movie with an all-star cast that included philosopher Ringo Starr.

Funny stuff—but, unfortunately, it all misconstrues Leibniz's thesis. Leibniz was a *rationalist*, a philosophical term-of-trade for someone who thinks that reason takes precedence over other ways of acquiring knowledge (as opposed, for example, to an *empiricist*, who maintains that the senses are the primary path to knowledge.) Leibniz got to his idea that this is the best of all possible worlds by arguing by reason alone that:

1. There would be no world at all if God had not chosen to create a world.
2. The "principle of sufficient reason" says that when there is more than one alternative, there must be an explanation for why one is the case rather than another.
3. In the case of God's choosing a particular world to create, the explanation must necessarily be found in the attributes of God himself, since there was nothing else around at the time.
4. Because God is both all-powerful and morally perfect, he must have created the *best* possible world. If you think about it, under the circumstances it was the *only* possible world. Being all-powerful and morally perfect, God could not have created a world that wasn't the best.

Voltaire, Bernstein et al, and Southern and Hoffenberg all satirize what they take to be Leibniz's meaning: "Everything is hunky-dory." But Leibniz didn't think there was no evil in the world. He merely thought that for God to have created the world in any other way would have resulted in even more evil.

Fortunately, we have a couple of jokes that actually *do* shed light on Leibniz's philosophy.

An optimist thinks that this is the best of all possible worlds. A pessimist fears that this is so.

The joke implies that the optimist approves of the idea that this is the best of all possible worlds, while the pessimist does not. From Leibniz's rationalist perspective, the world simply is what it is; the joke clarifies the obvious truth that optimism and pessimism are personal attitudes that have nothing to do with Leibniz's neutral, rational description of the world.

The optimist says, "The glass is half full."
The pessimist says, "The glass is half empty."
The rationalist says, "This glass is twice as big as it needs to be."

That makes it clear as glass.

Infinity and Eternity

It turns out that, however wonderful this world is or isn't, we're only here for a short visit. But short compared to what? An unlimited number of years?

The notion of infinity has been confounding metaphysicians

for, well, an eternity. Non-metaphysicians, however, have been less impressed.

> Two cows are standing in the pasture. One turns to the other and says, "Although *pi* is usually abbreviated to five numbers, it actually goes on into infinity."
> The second cow turns to the first and says, "Moo."

The following joke combines the idea of eternity with another howler of a philosophical concept, relativity:

> A woman is told by her doctor that she has six months to live. "Is there anything I can do?" she asks.
> "Yes, there is," the doctor replies. "You could marry a tax accountant."
> "How will that help my illness?" the woman asks.
> "Oh, it won't help your illness," says the doctor, "but it will make that six months seem like an eternity!"

This joke raises the philosophical question, "How could something finite, like six months, possibly be analogous to something infinite, like eternity?" Those who ask this question have never lived with a tax accountant.

Determinism versus Free Will

While we are in the here and now, do we have any control over our destiny?

Down through the centuries, much philosophical ink has been

Leibniz, being a rationalist, wasn't content to say that any-thing "just happened," as though something else might just as easily have happened instead. He felt that there must be some *reason* that made every situation *necessary*. Why does it rain more in Seattle than in Albuquerque? Because conditions A, B, and C make it *impossible* for it to be the other way around. Given conditions A, B, and C, it couldn't be any other way. So far most of us would agree with him, especially those of us who live in Seattle. But Liebniz goes on to argue that even those antecedent conditions (A, B, and C) could not have been otherwise. And the ones before them, and before them, and so on and so on and scooby-dooby-doo. This is what he called the "Principle of Sufficient Reason," meaning that the reason any actual state of affairs *is* actual is that it would be impossible for it to be otherwise. A universe that did not have a disproportionate amount of rain in Seattle *and all the conditions that lead to that rain* just wouldn't cut it as a universe. It would be chaos; the universe would have no "uni."

spilled over the question of whether human beings are free to decide and act or whether our decisions and actions are determined by external forces: heredity, environment, history, fate, Microsoft.

The Greek tragedians stressed the influence of character and its inevitable flaws in determining the course of events.

When asked whether he believed in free will, twentieth-century novelist Isaac Bashevis Singer replied, tongue-in-cheek, "I have no choice." (This is actually a position that some philosophers have taken with empty cheeks: that we are compelled to believe in our own free will because otherwise there is no basis for our belief in moral responsibility. Our moral choices would be out of our hands.)

Recently, the notion that psychological forces outside our control determine our behaviour has eroded the idea of moral responsibility to the point that we now have the "Twinkie defense," in which a defendant in San Francisco claimed that the sugar in his snack compelled him to commit murder. It's "the devil made me do it" dressed up in psychological garb.

Then again, there are some determinists who say, "God made me do it. In fact, God has determined everything in the universe down to the last detail." Baruch Spinoza, the seventeenth-century Dutch/Jewish philosopher, and Jonathan Edwards, the eighteenth-century American theologian, were proponents of this sort of theological determinism.

The eagle, the frog, and the truck driver in the following story all probably thought they chose and executed their actions freely.

Moses, Jesus, and a bearded old man are playing golf. Moses drives a long one, which lands on the fairway but rolls directly toward the pond. Moses raises his club, parts the water, and the ball rolls safely to the other side.

Jesus also hits a long one toward the same pond, but just as it's about to land in the centre, it hovers above the surface. Jesus casually walks out on the pond and chips it onto the green.

The bearded man's drive hits a fence and bounces out onto the street, where it rebounds off an oncoming truck and back onto the fairway. It's headed directly for the pond, but it lands on a lily pad, where a frog sees it and snatches it into his mouth. An eagle swoops down, grabs the frog, and flies away. As the eagle and frog pass over the green, the frog drops the ball, and it lands in the cup for a hole-in-one.

Moses turns to Jesus and says, "I hate playing with your dad."

Process Philosophy

It had to happen—a philosopher came along who took exception to this notion of a compulsive God who has his finger in everything. Twentieth-century philosopher Alfred North Whitehead argued that not only is God incapable of determining the future—the future will determine him. According to Whitehead's process philosophy, God is neither omnipotent nor omniscient, but is changed by events as they unfold. Or, as hippies might say, "God is, like, so evolved."

Alvin is working in his store when he hears a booming voice from above that says, "Alvin, sell your business!" He ignores it. The voice goes on for days saying, "Alvin, sell your business for three million dollars!" After weeks of this, he relents and sells his store.

The voice says, "Alvin, go to Las Vegas!"

Alvin asks why.

"Alvin, just take the three million dollars and go to Las Vegas."

Alvin obeys, goes to Las Vegas, and visits a casino.

The voice says, "Alvin, go to the blackjack table and put it all down on one hand!"

Alvin hesitates but gives in. He's dealt an eighteen. The dealer has a six showing.

"Alvin, take a card!"

"*What?* The dealer has . . ."

"Take a card!"

Alvin tells the dealer to hit him, and gets an ace. Nineteen. He breathes easy.

"Alvin, take another card."

"*What?*"

"TAKE ANOTHER CARD!"

Alvin asks for another card. It's another ace. He has twenty.

"Alvin, take another card!" the voice commands.

"*I have twenty!*" Alvin shouts.

"TAKE ANOTHER CARD!" booms the voice.

"*Hit me!*" Alvin says. He gets another ace. Twenty-one!

And the booming voice says, "Un-fucking-believable!"

Hey, there *is* something appealing about a God who can surprise himself.

The Principle of Parsimony

There has always been an antimetaphysical strain in philosophy, culminating in the triumph of the scientific worldview in the last two centuries. Rudolf Carnap and the Vienna Circle (not a seventies disco group, contrary to popular opinion) went so far as to outlaw metaphysics as nonrational speculation that has been superseded by science.

Rudy and the V.C. took their cue from the fourteenth-century theologian William Occam, who came up with the principle of parsimony, aka "Occam's razor." This principle declares that, "Theories should not be any more complex than necessary." Or, as Occam put it metaphysically, theories should not "multiply entities unnecessarily."

Suppose Isaac Newton had watched the apple fall and exclaimed, "I've got it! Apples are being caught in a tug-of-war between gremlins pulling them up and trolls pulling them down, and trolls are stronger!"

Occam would have retorted, "Okay, Isaac, so your theory does account for all the observable facts, but get with the programme—keep it simple!"

Carnap would agree.

One evening after dinner, a five-year-old boy asked his father, "Where did mother go?"

His father told him, "Your mother is at a Tupperware party."

This explanation satisfied the boy only for a moment, but then he asked, "What's a Tupperware party, Dad?"

His father figured a simple explanation would be the best approach. "Well, son," he said, "at a Tupperware party, a bunch of ladies sit around and sell plastic bowls to each other."

The boy burst out laughing. "Come on, Dad! What is it really?"

The simple truth is that a Tupperware party really *is* a bunch of ladies sitting around and selling plastic bowls to each other. But the marketing folks at the Tupperware Corporation, metaphysicians that they are, would have us believe it's more complex than that.

DIMITRI: I ask you one simple question, and you give me ten different answers. It's not exactly helpful.

TASSO: If it's help you want, go see a social worker. I hear they've got loads of them in Sparta.

DIMITRI: No, what I want to know is which answer is true?

TASSO: Aha! Now we're getting somewhere.

Logic

Without logic, reason is useless. With it, you can win arguments and alienate multitudes.

DIMITRI: There are so many competing philosophies. How can I be sure anything's true?

TASSO: Who says anything is true?

DIMITRI: There you go again. Why do you always answer a question with another question?

TASSO: You got a problem with that?

DIMITRI: I don't even know why I asked, because some things just are true. Like two plus two equals four. That's true, end of story.

TASSO: But how can you be sure?

DIMITRI: Because I am one smart Athenian.

TASSO: That's another question. But the reason you can be sure two plus two equals four is because it follows the irrefutable laws of logic.

The Law of Noncontradiction

Tasso's right.

Let's start off with a classic joke that draws on Aristotelian logic.

> A rabbi is holding court in his village. Schmuel stands up and pleads his case, saying, "Rabbi, Itzak runs his sheep across my land every day and it is ruining my crops. It's my land. It's not fair."
>
> The rabbi says, "You're right!"
>
> But then Itzak stands up and says, "But Rabbi, going across his land is the only way my sheep can drink water from the pond. Without it, they'll die. For centuries, every shepherd has had the right of way on the land surrounding the pond, so I should too."
>
> And the rabbi says, "You're right!"
>
> The cleaning lady, who has overheard all this, says to the rabbi, "But, Rabbi, they can't both be right!"
>
> And the rabbi replies, "You're right!"

The cleaning lady has informed the rabbi that he has violated Aristotle's Law of Noncontradiction, which for a rabbi isn't quite as bad as violating the law against coveting your neighbour's maidservant, but it's close. The Law of Noncontradiction says that nothing can both be so and not be so at the same time.

Illogical Reasoning

Illogical reasoning is the bane of philosophers, but heaven knows, it can be useful. That's probably why it's so prevalent.

An Irishman walks into a Dublin bar, orders three pints of Guinness, and drinks them down, taking a sip from one, then a sip from the next, until they're gone. He then orders three more. The bartender says, "You know, they'd be less likely to go flat if you bought them one at a time."

The man says, "Yeah, I know, but I have two brothers, one in the States, one in Australia. When we all went our separate ways, we promised each other that we'd all drink this way in memory of the days when we drank together. Each of these is for one of my brothers and the third is for me."

The bartender is touched, and says, "What a great custom!"

The Irishman becomes a regular in the bar and always orders the same way.

One day he comes in and orders two pints. The other regulars notice, and a silence falls over the bar. When he comes to the bar for his second round, the bartender says, "Please accept my condolences, pal."

The Irishman says, "Oh, no, everyone's fine. I just joined the Mormon Church, and I had to quit drinking."

In other words, self-serving logic can get you served.

Inductive Logic

Inductive logic reasons from particular instances to general theories and is the method used to confirm scientific theories. If you observe enough apples falling from trees, you will conclude that apples always fall down, instead of up or sideways. You might then form a more general hypothesis that includes other falling bodies, like pears. Thus is the progress of science.

In the annals of literature, no character is as renowned for his powers of "deduction" as the intrepid Sherlock Holmes, but the way Holmes operates is not generally by using deductive logic at all. He really uses inductive logic. First, he carefully observes the situation, then he generalizes from his prior experience, using analogy and probability, as he does in the following story:

Holmes and Watson are on a camping trip. In the middle of the night Holmes wakes up and gives Dr. Watson a nudge. "Watson," he says, "look up in the sky and tell me what you see."

"I see millions of stars, Holmes," says Watson.

"And what do you conclude from that, Watson?"

Watson thinks for a moment. "Well," he says, "astronomically, it tells me that there are millions of galaxies and potentially billions of planets. Astrologically, I observe that Saturn is in Leo. Horologically, I deduce that the time is approximately a quarter past three. Meteorologically, I suspect that we will have a beautiful day tomorrow. Theologically, I see that God is all-powerful, and we are small and insignificant. Uh, what does it tell you, Holmes?"

"Watson, you idiot! Someone has stolen our tent!"

We don't know exactly how Holmes arrived at his conclusion, but perhaps it was something like this:

1. I went to sleep in a tent, but now I can see the stars.

2. My intuitive working hypothesis, based on analogies to similar experiences I have had in the past, is that someone has stolen our tent.

3. In testing that hypothesis, let's rule out alternative hypotheses:

    a. Perhaps the tent is still here, but someone is projecting a picture of stars on the roof of the tent. This is unlikely, based on my past experience of human behaviour and the equipment that experience tells me would have to be present in the tent and obviously isn't.

    b. Perhaps the tent blew away. This is unlikely, as my past experiences lead me to conclude that that amount of wind would have awakened me, though perhaps not Watson.

    c. Etc., etc., etc.

4. No, I think my original hypothesis is probably correct. Someone has stolen our tent.

Induction. All these years we've been calling Holmes's skill by the wrong term.

Falsifiability

Patient: Last night I dreamt I had Jennifer Lopez and Angelina Jolie in bed, and the three of us made love all night.

Shrink: Obviously, you have a deep-seated desire to sleep with your mother.

Patient: What?! Neither of those women looks remotely like my mother.

AN INDUCTIVE LEAP?

"I mean, what sort of thief takes only a dog bowl?"

Shrink: Aha! A reaction formation! You're obviously repressing your *real* desires.

The above is *not* a joke—it is actually the way some Freudians reason. And the problem with their reasoning is that there is no conceivable set of actual circumstances that would disprove their Oedipal theory. In his critique of inductive logic, twentieth-century philosopher Karl Popper argued that in order for a theory to hold water, there must be some possible circumstances that could demonstrate it to be false. In the above pseudo joke, there are no such circumstances that the Freudian therapist will admit as evidence.

And here's a *real* joke that hits Popper's point even more pointedly:

Two men are making breakfast. As one is buttering the toast, he says, "Did you ever notice that if you drop a piece of toast, it always lands butter side down?"

The second guy says, "No, I bet it just seems that way because it's so unpleasant to clean up the mess when it lands butter side down. I bet it lands butter side up just as often."

The first guy says, "Oh, yeah? Watch this." He drops the toast to the floor, where it lands butter side up.

The second guy says, "See, I told you."

The first guy says, "Oh, I see what happened. I buttered the wrong side!"

For this guy, no amount of evidence will falsify his theory.

Deductive Logic

Deductive logic reasons from the general to the particular. The bare-bones deductive argument is the syllogism "All men are mortal; Socrates is a man; therefore, Socrates is a mortal." It's amazing how often people screw this up and argue something like, "All men are mortal; Socrates is mortal; therefore, Socrates is a man," which doesn't logically follow. That would be like saying, "All men are mortal; my kid's hamster is mortal; therefore, my kid's hamster is a man."

Another way to screw up a deductive argument is by arguing from a false premise.

An old cowboy goes into a bar and orders a drink. As he sits there sipping his whisky, a young lady sits down next to him. She turns to the cowboy and asks him, "Are you a real cowboy?"

He replies, "Well, I've spent my whole life on the ranch, herding horses, mending fences, and branding cattle, so I guess I am."

She says, "I'm a lesbian. I spend my whole day thinking about women. As soon as I get up in the morning, I think about women. When I shower or watch TV, everything seems to make me think of women."

A little while later, a couple sits down next to the old cowboy and asks him, "Are you a real cowboy?"

He replies, "I always thought I was, but I just found out I'm a lesbian."

Perhaps it would be fun to analyze exactly where the cowboy went wrong. Perhaps not. But we're going to do it anyhow.

In his first answer to the question of whether he is a real cowboy, he reasoned,

1. If someone spends all his time doing cowboy-type things, he is a real cowboy.
2. I spend all my time doing those cowboy-type things.
3. Therefore, I am a real cowboy.

The woman reasoned,

1. If a woman spends all her time thinking about women, she is a lesbian.
2. I am a woman.
3. I spend all my time thinking about women.
4. Therefore, I am a lesbian.

When the cowboy then reasons to the same conclusion, he assumes a premise that in his case is false: namely, (2) I am a woman.

Okay, we never promised you that philosophy is the *same* as jokes.

The Inductive Argument from Analogy

There's nothing like an argument from analogy. Well, maybe a duck. One use of the argument from analogy is found in response to the question of what or who created the universe. Some have argued that because the universe is like a clock, there must be a Clockmaker. As the eighteenth-century British empiricist David Hume pointed out, this is a slippery argument, because there is nothing that is really perfectly analogous to the universe as a whole, unless it's another universe, so we shouldn't try to pass off anything that is just a part of *this* universe. Why a clock anyhow? Hume asks. Why not say the universe is analogous to a kangaroo? After all, both are organically interconnected systems. But the kangaroo analogy would lead to a very different conclusion about the origin of the universe: namely, that it was born of another universe after that universe had sex with a third universe. A fundamental problem with arguments from analogy is the assumption that, because some aspects of A are similar to B, other aspects of A are similar to B. It ain't necessarily so.

Recently, the clockwork argument has staged a comeback as the "theory" of Intelligent Design, which proposes that the supercomplexity of stuff in nature (think snowflakes, eyeballs, quarks) proves that there must be a superintelligent designer. When the Dover, Pennsylvania, Board of Education was challenged for including Intelligent Design as an "alternate theory" to evolution in their school curriculum, the presiding judge, John Jones III, ruled, in effect, that they should go back to school. In his often wittily written opinion, Jones could not restrain himself from poking fun at some of the defense's so-called expert witnesses, like one professor who admitted that the argument from analogy was flawed, but "it still works in science-fiction movies." Next witness, please!

Another problem with arguments from analogy is that you get totally different analogies from different points of view.

Three engineering students are discussing what sort of God must have designed the human body. The first says, "God must be a mechanical engineer. Look at all the joints."

The second says, "I think God must be an electrical engineer. The nervous system has thousands of electrical connections."

The third says, "Actually, God is a civil engineer. Who else would run a toxic waste pipeline through a recreational area?"

Ultimately arguments from analogy are not very satisfying. They don't provide the kind of certainty we would like when it comes to basic beliefs like the existence of God. There is nothing worse than a philosopher's bad analogy, except perhaps a school pupil's. Witness the results of the "Worst Analogies Ever Written in a High School Essay" contest, run by *The Washington Post*:

- "Long separated by cruel fate, the star-crossed lovers raced across the grassy field toward each other like two freight trains, one having left Cleveland at 6:36 p.m. traveling at 55 m.p.h., the other from Topeka at 7:47 pr.m. at a speed of 35 m.p.h."

- "John and Mary had never met. They were like two hummingbirds who had also never met."

- "The little boat gently drifted across the pond exactly the way a bowling ball wouldn't."

- "From the attic came an unearthly howl. The whole scene had an eerie, surreal quality, like when you're on vacation in another city and *Jeopardy* comes on at 7 p.m. instead of 7:30."

The "post hoc ergo propter hoc" Fallacy

First, a word about the social usage of this term: In some circles, when uttered with a straight face, this phrase can help you get lucky at a party. Interestingly, it has the exact opposite effect when uttered in English: "After this, therefore because of this." Go figure.

The phrase describes the error of assuming that because one thing *follows* another, that thing was *caused* by the other. For obvious reasons, this false logic is popular in sociopolitical discourse, such as "Most people hooked on heroin started with marijuana." True, but even more started with milk.

Post hoc makes life more entertaining in some cultures:

"The sun rises when the cockerel crows, so the cockerel's crowing must make the sun rise." Thanks, cockerel! Or take our colleague:

Every morning, she steps out onto her front porch and exclaims, "Let this house be safe from tigers!" Then she goes back inside.

Finally, we said to her, "What's that all about? There isn't a tiger within a thousand miles of here."

And she said, "See? It works!"

Post hoc jokes have multiplied in direct proportion to human delusions.

An older Jewish gentleman marries a younger lady, and they are very much in love. However, no matter what the husband does sexually, the woman never reaches orgasm. Since a Jewish wife is entitled to sexual pleasure, they decide to ask the rabbi. The rabbi listens to their story, strokes his beard, and makes the following suggestion:

"Hire a strapping young man. While the two of you are making love, have the young man wave a towel over you. That will help the wife fantasize and should bring on an orgasm."

They go home and follow the rabbi's advice. They hire a handsome young man and he waves a towel over them as they make love. It doesn't help, and she is still unsatisfied.

Perplexed, they go back to the rabbi. "Okay," says the rabbi to the husband, "let's try it reversed. Have the young man make love to your wife and you wave the towel over them." Once again, they follow the rabbi's advice.

The young man gets into bed with the wife, and the husband waves the towel. The young man gets to work with great enthusiasm and the wife soon has an enormous, room-shaking, screaming orgasm.

The husband smiles, looks at the young man and says to him triumphantly, "Schmuck, *that's* the way you wave a towel!"

Okay, one last *post hoc* joke. Promise.

An octogenarian man in a nursing home comes up to an elderly lady wearing hot pink capri pants and says, "Today's my birthday!"

"Wonderful," she replies. "I bet I can tell you exactly how old you are."

"Really? How?"

The lady says, "Easy. Drop your trousers."

The man drops his trousers.

"Okay," she says, "now drop your pants."

The man does her bidding. She fondles him a moment and says, "You're eighty-four!"

He says, "How did you know that?"

And she says, "You told me yesterday."

The old man has fallen for the oldest trick in the book, *post hoc ergo propter hoc,* or *after* she copped a feel, *therefore because* she copped a feel... It's that *propter* part that gets you every time.

In general, we're deceived by *post hoc ergo propter hoc* because we fail to notice that there's another cause at work.

A New York boy is being led through the swamps of Louisiana by his cousin. "Is it true that an alligator won't attack you if you carry a flashlight?" asks the city boy.
His cousin replies, "Depends on how fast you carry the flashlight."

The city boy saw the flashlight as a *propter* when it was only a prop.

Monte Carlo Fallacy

Gamblers will recognize the Monte Carlo Fallacy. Some may be surprised to hear it's a fallacy. They may be treating it as the Monte Carlo Strategy. Actually, croupiers depend upon that.

We know that a roulette wheel that has half red positions and half black positions has a 50 percent chance of stopping on red. If we turn the wheel a large number of times—say 1,000—and the wheel isn't rigged or otherwise faulty, on average it should stop on red 500 times. So, if we turn the wheel six times and it stops on black all six times, we are tempted to think that the odds are in our favour if we play red on the seventh turn. Red is "due," right? Wrong. The wheel has exactly the same 50 percent chance of stopping on red on the seventh turn as it had on every other turn, and this would be true no matter how many blacks had come up in a row.

Here's some sage advice based on the Monte Carlo Fallacy:

If you are getting on a commercial airliner, for safety's sake, take a bomb with you . . . because the overwhelming odds are there won't be two guys on the same plane with a bomb.

Circular Argument

A circular argument is an argument in which the evidence for a proposition contains the proposition itself. Often a circular argument can be a joke all by itself, with no adornment necessary.

It was autumn, and the Native Americans on the reservation asked their new chief if it was going to be a cold winter. Raised in the ways of the modern world, the chief had never been taught the old secrets and had no way of knowing whether the winter would be cold or mild. To be on the safe side, he advised the tribe to collect wood and be prepared for a cold winter. A few days later, as a practical afterthought, he called the National Weather Service and asked whether they were forecasting a cold winter. The meteorologist replied that, indeed, he thought the winter would be quite cold. The chief advised the tribe to stock even more wood.

A couple of weeks later, the chief checked in again with the Weather Service. "Does it still look like a cold winter?" asked the chief.

"It sure does," replied the meteorologist. "It looks like a *very* cold winter." The chief advised the tribe to gather up every scrap of wood they could find.

A couple of weeks later, the chief called the Weather Service again and asked how the winter was looking at that point. The meteorologist said, "We're now forecasting that it will be one of the coldest winters on record!"

"Really?" said the chief. "How can you be so sure?"

The meteorologist replied, "The Native Americans are collecting wood like crazy!"

The chief's evidence for the need to stock more wood turns out to be that he was stocking more wood. Fortunately, he was using a circular saw.

Argument from Respect for Authority (Argumentum ad Verecundiam) Fallacy

The argument from respect for authority is one of our boss's favourite arguments. Citing an authority to support your argument is not a logical fallacy in and of itself; expert opinion is legitimate evidence alongside other evidence. What *is* fallacious is using respect for authority as the sole confirmation of your position, despite convincing evidence to the contrary.

Ted meets his friend Al and exclaims, "Al! I heard you died!"

"Hardly," says Al, laughing. "As you can see, I'm very much alive."

"Impossible," says Ted. "The man who told me is much more reliable than you."

What is always at play in arguments from authority is whom one accepts as a legitimate authority.

A man walks into a pet shop and asks to see the parrots. The shop owner shows him two beautiful ones out on the floor. "This one is £5,000 and the other is £10,000," he says.

"Wow!" says the man. "What does the £5,000 one do?"

"This parrot can sing every aria Mozart wrote," says the shop owner.

"And the other?"

"He sings Wagner's entire *Ring* cycle. There's another parrot out back for £30,000."

"Holy moley! What does he do?"

"Nothing that I've heard, but the other two call him 'Maestro.'"

According to our authorities, some authorities have better credentials than others; the problem arises when the other side doesn't accept those credentials.

Four rabbis used to argue theology together, and three were always in accord against the fourth. One day, the odd rabbi out, after losing three to one again, decided to appeal to a higher authority.

"O, God!" he cried. "I know in my heart that I am right and they are wrong! Please give me a sign to prove it to them!"

It was a beautiful, sunny day. As soon as the rabbi finished his prayer, a storm cloud moved across the sky above the four rabbis. It rumbled once and dissolved. "A sign from God! See, I'm right, I knew it!" But the other three disagreed, pointing out that storm clouds often form on hot days.

So the rabbi prayed again. "O, God, I need a bigger sign to show that I am right and they are wrong. So please, God, a bigger sign!" This time four storm clouds appeared, rushed toward each other to form one big cloud, and a bolt of lightning slammed into a tree on a nearby hill.

"I told you I was right!" cried the rabbi, but his friends insisted that nothing had happened that could not be explained by natural causes.

The rabbi was getting ready to ask for a very, very big sign, but just as he said, "O, God . . . ," the sky turned pitch-black, the earth shook, and a deep, booming voice intoned, "HEEEEEEEE'S RIIIIIIGHT!"

The rabbi put his hands on his hips, turned to the other three, and said, "Well?"

"So," shrugged one of the other rabbis, "now it's three to two."

Zeno's Paradox

A paradox is a seemingly sound piece of reasoning based on seemingly true assumptions that leads to a contradiction or another obviously false conclusion. In slightly different words, this could be the definition of a joke—at least, most of the jokes in this book. There's something absurd about true stuff that leads ever so logically to false stuff; and absurd is funny. Holding two mutually contradicting ideas in our heads at the same time makes us giddy. But most significantly, you can tell a tricky paradox at a party and get a good laugh.

When it comes to holding two mutually exclusive ideas simultaneously, Zeno of Elea was a real clown. Have you heard his story about the race between Achilles and the tortoise? Naturally, Achilles can run faster than the tortoise, so the tortoise is given a big head start. At the gun—or as they said in the fifth century B.C., at the javelin—Achilles's first goal is to get to the point where the tortoise started. Of course, by then the tortoise has moved a little way. So now Achilles has to get to *that* spot. By the time he gets there, the tortoise has moved again. No matter how many times Achilles reaches the tortoise's prior location, even if he does it an infinite number of times, Achilles will never catch up with the tortoise, although he'll get awfully close. All the tortoise needs to do to win the race is to not to stop.

Okay, so Zeno isn't Leno, but he's not bad for a fifth-century B.C. philosopher. And, like the classic stand-up comedians of yore, Zeno can say, "I've got a million of 'em." Well, actually, only four. Another was his racetrack paradox. In order to get to the end of the racetrack, a runner must first complete an infinite number of journeys. He must run to the midpoint; then he must run to the midpoint of the remaining distance; then to the midpoint of the still remaining distance, etc., etc. Theoretically speaking, because he has to get to mid-points an infinite number of times, he can never get to the end of the track. But of course he does. Even Zeno can see that.

Here's an old comedy routine that seems to come straight out of Zeno:

> Salesman: Madam, this vacuum cleaner will cut your work in half."
> Customer: "Terrific! Give me two of them."

There's a weird thing about this joke. The racetrack paradox runs counter to common sense, and even if we can't figure out what's wrong with it, we're confident that *something* is. In the vacuum cleaner joke though, Zeno's reasoning is not paradoxical at all. If the woman's goal is to get the work done in no time at all, no number of time-saving vacuum cleaners (and people to run them concurrently with her) is going to do it. Running two vacuums will only cut the rug-cleaning time by three quarters; running three, by five sixths; and so on, as the number of vacuum cleaners goes on to infinity.

Logical and Semantic Paradoxes

The mother of all the logical and semantic paradoxes was Russell's paradox, named for its author, twentieth-century English philosopher Bertrand Russell. It goes like this: "Is the set of all sets that are not members of themselves a member of itself?" This one is a real screamer—that is, if you happen to have an advanced degree in mathematics. But hang on. Fortunately, two other twentieth-century logicians named Grelling and Nelson came along with a more accessible version of Russell's paradox. It's a semantic paradox that operates on the concept of words that refer to themselves.

Here goes: There are two kinds of words, those that refer to themselves (autological) and those that don't (heterological). Some examples of autological words are "short" (which is a short word), "polysyllabic" (which has several syllables), and our favourite, "seventeen-lettered" (which has seventeen letters). Examples of heterological words are "knock-kneed" (a word that has no knees, touching or otherwise) and "monosyllabic" (a word that has more than one syllable). The question is: Is the word "heterological" autological or heterological? If it's autological, then it's heterological. If it's heterological, then it's autological. Ha! Ha!

Still not laughing? Well, here's another case where translating a philosophical concept into a funny story makes it clearer:

There is a town in which the sole barber—a man, by the way—shaves all the townsmen, and only those townsmen, who do not shave themselves. Does the barber shave himself?

If he does, he doesn't. If he doesn't, he does.

Now that's Russell's paradox for the party set.

We don't often visit women's toilets, so we can't be sure what goes on in there, but we do know that male readers will be familiar with the paradoxes often scribbled on the walls of men's room stalls, especially in universities. They are logical/semantic paradoxes along the lines of Russell's and Grelling-Nelson's, but snappier. Remember these? Remember where you were sitting at the time?

True or false: "This sentence is false."

Or,

If a man tries to fail and succeeds, which did he do?

Just for fun, inscribe, "Is the word 'heterological' autological or heterological?" over the urinal next time you drop by. It's a classy thing to do.

DIMITRI: Cute. But what does any of this have to do with answering the Big Questions?

TASSO: Well, let's say you visit the Oracle at Delphi and ask him, "What's it all about, Delphi?" And he answers, "Life is a picnic; all picnics are fun: therefore, life is fun." Logic gives you something to chat about.

Epistemology:
The Theory of Knowledge

How do you know that you know the stuff you think you know? Take away the option of answering, "I just do!" and what's left is epistemology.

DIMITRI: I'm feeling good now, Tasso. I've got logic down cold, so the rest should be a picnic in the Acropolis.

TASSO: What Acropolis?

DIMITRI: That one! Right over there! Maybe you ought to ease off on the ouzo, pal.

TASSO: But is that the Acropolis or just something that you *believe* is the Acropolis? How do you know it's real? For that matter, how do you know *anything* is real?

DIMITRI: Next round's on me.

Reason vs. Revelation

So how *do* we know anything at all, if in fact we do know anything at all?

During the Middle Ages this question boiled down to whether divine revelation trumps reason as a source of human knowledge or vice versa.

A man stumbles into a deep well and plummets a hundred feet before grasping a spindly root, stopping his fall. His grip grows weaker and weaker, and in his desperation he cries out, "Is there anybody up there?"

He looks up, and all he can see is a circle of sky. Suddenly, the clouds part and a beam of bright light shines down on him. A deep voice thunders, "I, the Lord, am here. Let go of the root, and I will save you."

The man thinks for a moment and then yells, "Is there anybody else up there?"

Hanging by a root has a tendency to tip the scales toward reason.

In the seventeenth century, René Descartes opted for reason over a divine source of knowledge. This came to be known as putting Descartes before the source.

Descartes probably wishes he'd never said, *"Cogito ergo sum"* ("I think, therefore I am"), because it's all anybody ever remembers about him—that and the fact that he said it while sitting inside a bread oven. As if that weren't bad enough, his *"cogito"* is constantly misinterpreted to mean that Descartes believed thinking is an essential characteristic of being human. Well, actually, he did believe that, but that has nothing whatsoever to do with *cogito ergo sum*. Descartes arrived at the *cogito* through an experiment in radical doubt to discover if there was anything he could be certain of; that is, anything that he could not doubt away. He started out by doubting the existence of the external world. That was easy enough. Perhaps he was dreaming or hallucinating. Then he tried doubting his own existence. But doubt as he would, he kept coming up against the fact that there was a doubter. Must be himself! He could not doubt his own doubting. He could have saved himself a lot of misinterpretation if only he had said, *"Dubito ergo sum."*

Every American criminal-trial judge asks the jury to mimic Descartes's process of looking for certainty by testing the assertion of the defendant's guilt against a standard almost as high as Descartes's. The question for the jury is not identical to Descartes's; the judge does not ask whether the defendant's guilt is open to *any* doubt, but only whether it is open to *reasonable* doubt. But even this lower standard demands that the jury carry out a similar—and nearly as radical—mental experiment as Descartes did.

A defendant was on trial for murder. There was strong evidence indicating his guilt, but there was no corpse. In his closing statement, the defense attorney resorted to a trick. "Ladies and gentlemen of the jury," he said. "I have a surprise for you all—within one minute, the person presumed dead will walk into this courtroom."

He looked toward the courtroom door. The jurors, stunned, all looked eagerly. A minute passed. Nothing happened. Finally the lawyer said, "Actually, I made up the business about the dead man walking in. But you all looked at the door with anticipation. I therefore put it to you that there is reasonable doubt in this case as to whether anyone was killed, and I must insist that you return a verdict of 'not guilty.'"

The jury retired to deliberate. A few minutes later, they returned and pronounced a verdict of "guilty."

"But how could you do that?" bellowed the lawyer. "You must have had some doubt. I saw all of you stare at the door."

The jury foreman replied, "Oh, we looked, but your client didn't."

Empiricism

According to the eighteenth-century Irish empiricist Bishop George Berkeley, *"Esse est percipi"* ("To be is to be perceived"), which is to say that the so-called objective world is all in the mind. Berkeley argued that our only knowledge of this world is what comes to us through our senses. (Philosophers call this information "sense data.") Beyond these sense data, Berkeley said, you cannot infer anything else, such as the existence of substances out there sending out vibes that stimulate our senses. But the good bishop did go on to infer that sense data *has* to come from somewhere, so that *somewhere* must be God. Basically, Berkeley's idea is that God is up there tapping out sense data on a cosmic website to which we are all tuned in 24/7. (And we always thought God only worked 24/6!)

The story goes that Berkeley's contemporary, Dr. Samuel Johnson, upon being told of the "*Esse est percipi*" theory, kicked a hitching post, exclaiming, "Thus do I refute Bishop Berkeley!"

To Berkeley, it would have sounded like a gag. That kick and the sore toe that followed from it only proved that God was busy at his task of sending coordinated sense data Dr. Johnson's way: first, the sensation of foot motion stopping, followed immediately by the sensation of pain.

Things get more complicated when the source of our sense data is another human being:

A man is worried that his wife is losing her hearing, so he consults a doctor. The doctor suggests that he try a simple at-home test on her: Stand behind her and ask her a question, first from twenty feet away, next from ten feet, and finally right behind her.

So the man goes home and sees his wife in the kitchen facing the stove. He says from the door, "What's for dinner tonight?"

No answer.

Ten feet behind her, he repeats, "What's for dinner tonight?"

Still no answer.

Finally, right behind her he says, "What's for dinner tonight?"

And his wife turns around and says, "For the third time— chicken!"

Now, what this couple has is a serious sense-data interpretation problem.

Scientific Method

Today it seems like a no-brainer that all knowledge of the external world comes through our senses. But it was not always so. Many philosophers in bygone eras thought that there were some innate ideas in our minds that were there *a priori*—or prior to experience. Some thought our ideas of God were innate; others claimed that our idea of causality was innate too.

Even today, when someone says, "Everything happens for a reason," or "I believe in reincarnation," they are making a statement that cannot be either confirmed or disconfirmed by experience. But most of us accept that the best evidence for the truth of a statement about the external world is sensory experience, and in that sense we are all empiricists. That is, unless we are the King of Poland, the exception that proves the rule:

The King of Poland and a retinue of dukes and earls went out for a royal elk hunt. Just as they approached the woods, a serf came running out from behind a tree, waving his arms excitedly and yelling, "I am not an elk!"

The king took aim and shot the serf through the heart, killing him instantly.

"Good sire," a duke said, "why did you do that? He said he was not an elk."

"Dear me," the king replied. "I thought he said he was an elk."

All right, now let's compare the king with a hot-shot scientist.

A scientist and his wife are out for a drive in the country. The wife says, "Oh, look! Those sheep have been shorn."

"Yes," says the scientist. "On this side."

At first, we might think that the wife is only expressing a commonsense view, while the scientist is taking a more cautious, more scientific view, in that he refuses to go beyond the evidence of his senses. But we would be wrong. It is actually the wife who has formulated what most scientists would consider the more scientific hypothesis. The "experience" of empiricists is not restricted to direct sensory experience. Scientists use their *prior* experiences to calculate probabilities and to infer more general statements. What the wife is in effect saying is, "What I see are sheep that are shorn, at least on this side. From prior experience I know that farmers do not generally shear sheep only on one side and that, even if this farmer did, the probability of the sheep arranging themselves on the hillside so that only their shorn sides face the road is infinitesimal. Therefore, I feel confident saying, 'Those sheep have been completely shorn.'"

We assume that the scientist in the joke is some sort of over-educated egghead. More typically, we assume that a person who cannot extrapolate from his prior experience is simply a dunce, or, as they say in India, a Sardar.

A New Delhi policeman is interrogating three Sardars who are training to become detectives. To test their skills in recognizing a suspect, he shows the first Sardar a picture for five seconds and then hides it. "This is your suspect. How would you recognize him?"

The Sardar answers, "That's easy, we'll catch him fast because he only has one eye!"

The policeman says, "Sardar! That's because the picture I showed you is his profile."

Then the policeman flashes the picture for five seconds at the second Sardar and asks him, "This is your suspect. How would you recognize him?"

The second Sardar smiles and says, "Ha! He'd be too easy to catch because he only has one ear!"

The policeman angrily responds, "What's the matter with you two? Of course only one eye and one ear are showing, because it's a picture of his profile! Is that the best answer you can come up with?"

Extremely frustrated at this point, he shows the picture to the third Sardar and in a very testy voice asks, "This is your suspect. How would you recognize him?"

The Sardar looks at the picture intently for a moment and says, "The suspect wears contact lenses." The policeman is caught off guard because he really doesn't know whether the suspect wears contact lenses. "Well, that's an interesting answer," he says. "Wait here for a few minutes while I check his file and I'll get back to you on that."

He leaves the room, goes to his office, checks the suspect's file in his computer, and comes back smiling. "Wow! I can't believe it. It's true! The suspect does in fact wear contact lenses. Good work! How were you able to make such an astute observation?"

"That's easy," the Sardar replied. "He can't wear regular glasses because he only has one eye and one ear."

The triumph of empiricism in Western epistemology is reflected in the fact that we automatically assume it to be the method of verification everyone uses:

Three women are in a locker room dressing to play squash when a man runs through wearing nothing but a bag over his head. The first woman looks at his willy and says, "Well, it's not my husband." The second woman says, "No, it isn't." The third says, "He's not even a member of this club."

Still, despite the triumph of empiricism and science, many people continue to interpret some unusual events as miraculous rather than the result of natural causes. David Hume, the sceptical British empiricist, said that the only rational basis for believing that something is a miracle is that all alternative explanations are even more improbable. Say a man insists he has a potted palm that sings arias from *Aida*. Which is more improbable: that the potted palm has violated the laws of nature, or that the man is crazy, or fibbing or high on mushrooms? Hume's response: "Puh-*leez*!" (We're paraphrasing here.) Since the odds of the man having been deceived or having stretched the truth are always somewhat greater than the odds of a violation of the laws of nature, Hume could foresee no circumstance in which it would be rational to conclude that a miracle had happened.

Add to this the generally known fact that potted palms prefer Puccini to Verdi.

Interestingly, in the following story, Bill, an apparent student of Hume, puts a presumed miracle to the test, but in the end is driven to the conclusion that the alternative explanation is *even more* unlikely:

One day Anup complained to his friend that his elbow really hurt. His friend suggested that he visit a swami who lived in a nearby cave. "Simply leave a sample of urine outside his cave, and he will meditate on it, miraculously diagnose your problem, and tell you what you can do about it. It only costs five hundred rupees."

Anup figured he had little to lose, so he filled a jar with urine and left it outside the cave with a five hundreed rupee note. The next day when he came back, there was a note waiting for him that said, "You have tennis elbow. Soak your arm in warm water. Avoid heavy lifting. It will be better in two weeks."

Later that evening, Anup started to think that the swami's "miracle" was a put-up job by his friend, who could have written the note and left it outside the cave himself. So Anup decided to get back at his friend. He mixed together some tap water, a yard sample from his dog, and urine samples from his wife and son. To top it off, he included another bodily fluid of his own, and left the concoction outside the cave with five hundred rupees. He then called his friend and told him that he was having some other health problems and that he had left another sample for the swami.

The next day he returned to the cave and found another note that said, "Your tap water is too hard. Get a water softener. Your dog has worms. Get him vitamins. Your son is hooked on cocaine. Get him into rehab. Your wife is pregnant with twin girls. They aren't yours. Get a lawyer. And if you don't stop playing with yourself, your tennis elbow will never get better."

But usually in jokes, as in philosophy, the skeptical interpretation prevails.

Old "Doc" Bloom, the local hardware shop owner, who was known for his miraculous cures for arthritis, had a long line of "patients" waiting outside his door, when a little old lady, completely bent over, shuffled in slowly, leaning on her cane.

When her turn came, she went into the back room of the shop and, amazingly, emerged within half an hour, walking completely erect with her head held high.

A woman waiting in the line said, "It's a miracle! You walked in bent in half and now you're walking erect. What did Doc do?"

She answered, "He gave me a longer cane."

A blind man can obviously be as much of an empiricist as the next guy, though visual data will not figure in his experience:

It's Passover and a Jewish guy is eating his lunch in the park. A blind man sits down next to him, so the Jewish guy offers him some of his lunch—a piece of matzoh. The blind man takes it, fingers it a moment, and says, "Who writes this crap?"

The man in the following story makes the absurd mistake of assuming that a blind man would have no other means of sensory verification:

A man goes into a bar with his dog and asks for a drink. The bartender says, "You can't bring that dog in here!" The guy, without missing a beat, says, "This is my guide dog."

"Oh, I'm sorry, man," says the bartender. "Here, the first one's on me." The man takes his drink and goes to a table near the door.

Another guy walks into the bar with a dog. The first guy stops him and says, "You can't bring that dog in here unless you tell him it's a guide dog." The second man graciously thanks him, continues to the bar, and asks for a drink. The bartender says, "Hey, you can't bring that dog in here!"

The man replies, "This is my guide dog."

The bartender says, "No, I don't think so. They don't use Chihuahuas as guide dogs."

The man pauses for a half-second and replies, "What?!?! They gave me a Chihuahua?!?"

German Idealism

Oh, come on! There's gotta be more to an object than just sense data. Maybe behind it somewhere.

The eighteenth-century German philosopher Immanuel Kant thought so. He read the British empiricists, and as he put it, they awakened him from his dogmatic slumber. Kant had assumed that our minds can provide us with certainty of what the world is really like. But the empiricists demonstrated that, because our knowledge of the external world comes to us through our senses, it is always, in a certain sense, uncertain. A strawberry is only red or sweet when it is observed through certain equipment—our eyes and our taste buds. We know that some people with different taste buds may not experience it as sweet at all. So, Kant asked, what is a strawberry "in itself" that makes it appear red and sweet—or otherwise—when run through our sensory equipment?

We may think that science can tell us what a thing *really is in itself*, even if our senses can't. But, when you think about it, science doesn't really get us any closer to the strawberry-in-itself. It doesn't actually help to say that a certain chemical makeup of the strawberry and a certain neurological makeup of a person combine to determine whether the strawberry appears sweet or tart—and that this chemical makeup is what the strawberry is "really" like in itself. What we mean by "a certain chemical make-up" is merely "the effect we observe when we run the strawberry through certain gizmos." Running the strawberry through the gizmos merely tells us how a strawberry appears when it's run through those gizmos, just as biting into one tells how us how one appears when it's run past our taste buds.

Kant concluded that we can know nothing about things as they are in themselves. The *ding an sich*, the thing-in-itself, he said, is "equal to x." We can only know the *phenomenal* world, the world of appearances; we can know nothing of the transcendent, *noumenal* world behind the appearances.

In so saying, Kant laid down the gauntlet for a paradigm shift in philosophy. Reason cannot tell us about the world beyond our senses. Neither Berkeley's God-as-data-entry-clerk or any metaphysical explanation of the world can be arrived at by pure reason. Philosophy was never the same again.

Secretary: Doctor, there's an invisible man in the waiting room.
Doctor: Tell him I can't see him.

You may not have found this joke completely helpful in explaining Kant's distinction between the phenomenal and the noumenal. That's because it loses something in translation. Here's how we originally heard the joke in a rathskeller at the University of Königsberg:

Secretary: Herr Doktor, there's a *ding an sich* in the waiting room.
Urologist: Another *ding an sich*! If I see one more today, I think I'm screaming! Who is it?
Secretary: How would I know?
Urologist: Describe him.
Secretary: You must be kidding!

There you have it: the original *sich* joke.

There's more going on in this joke than meets the eye. The secretary has chosen, for reasons best known to herself, not to share with the doctor her evidence that there's a *ding an sich* in the waiting room. Whatever that evidence was, it must have been phenomenal! (If you follow our drift.) What tipped her off? Must have been something in the realm of the senses. Maybe it was a *sixth* sense, maybe it was just senses one through five, but it was certainly a sense in some sense. The back story here is that the secretary had done her doctoral dissertation on Kant's *Critique of Pure Reason* prior to discovering that she had thereby limited her career options to secretary and fry chef. She therefore interpreted the doctor's demand, "Describe him," to mean not "What sensory phenomena are you experiencing?" but rather "Describe him as he is in himself, behind the appearances." She was understandably vexed by this demand, though she later recovered and went on to wed the doctor's cousin, Helmut, and raise three lovely children.

For Kant, and for much of epistemology that followed after him, the questions of what we can know and how we can know it can be analyzed in terms of what we can *say meaningfully* about what we know and how we know it. *What kinds of statements about the world contain knowledge of the world?*

Kant went about the task of answering this question by dividing statements into two categories: analytic and synthetic. Analytic statements are those that are true by definition.

The statement, "All platypuses are mammals" is analytic. It tells us nothing new about any actual platypus beyond what we could find out by simply looking up "platypus" in a dictionary. "Some platypuses are cross-eyed," on the other hand, is synthetic. It does give us new information about the world, because "cross-eyed" is not part of the definition of "platypus." "Some platypuses are cross-eyed" tells us something about platypuses that we couldn't find out by looking up "platypus" in a dictionary.

Next, Kant distinguished between *a priori* and *a posteriori* statements. *A priori* statements are those we are able to make on the basis of reason alone, without recourse to sensory experience. Our earlier statement, "All platypuses are mammals," is known *a priori*. We don't need to go look at a bunch of platypuses to see that it is true. We simply need to look in the dictionary. *A posteriori* judgments, on the other hand, are based on sensory experience of the world. "Some platypuses are cross-eyed" can be known only by checking out a number of platypuses—either checking them out ourselves or taking the word of someone who says they have.

So far we've seen examples of analytic *a priori* statements ("All platypuses are mammals") and synthetic *a posteriori* statements ("Some platypuses are cross-eyed"). Kant asked, "Is there a third type of statement, synthetic *a*

Portrait of a ding an sich

priori?" These would be statements that give us new knowledge about the external world, but that can be known by reason alone. The empiricists had implied that there is no synthetic *a priori* knowledge, since our source for knowledge of the external world is our sensory experience. But Kant said, "Hold the phone! How about statements like, 'Every event has a cause'?" It's synthetic: it tells us something new about the world beyond what is contained in the definitions of "cause" and "event." But it is also *a priori*, known by reason alone, not by experience. How so? "Because," said Kant, "it *has* to be assumed to be true if we are even to *have* intelligible experience." If we didn't assume that the present situation is caused by a chain of preceding events, we couldn't make sense out of anything. It would be like living in the film *Mulholland Drive*, where events occur in no coherent order. We'd have to forget about making *any* kind of statement or judgment about the world because we couldn't count on the world to be consistent from one minute to the next.

Hundreds of jokes hinge on confusing analytic *a priori* statements with synthetic *a posteriori* statements:

There's a surefire way to live to a ripe old age—eat a meatball a day for a hundred years.

The joke lies in giving an analytic, *a priori* "solution" to a problem that asks for a synthetic, *a posteriori* solution. The question of a surefire way to longevity clearly asks for some information about the world. "What are the things that *experience* has shown lead to longevity?" We expect the answer to be something like "Give up smoking" or "Take 400 milligrams of Co-Enzyme Q-10 at bedtime." But here the answer is analytic, with a little irrelevancy about meatballs thrown in to fog your mind. "To live to an old age, live a hundred years, because a hundred years is, by common definition, an old age. Eat some meatballs too. They can't hurt you." (Well, maybe all those trans-fats in the meatballs *could* hurt, but not, of course, if you eat them for a hundred years.)

Here's another:

Joe: What a fabulous singer, huh?
Dave: Ha! If I had his voice, I'd be just as good.

Same deal. What we *mean* by "fabulous singer" is one who possesses a terrific voice—the kind the performer in question obviously must have. So Blow's statement "If I had his voice, I'd be just as good" doesn't tell us anything new about Blow's singing abilities. All he is really saying is, "If I were a fabulous singer, I'd be a fabulous singer." And if that's not true by definition, nothing is.

Here's a more complicated demonstration of what happens

when you confuse synthetic *a posteriori* and analytic *a priori* statements:

> A man tries on a made-to-order suit and says to the tailor, "I need this sleeve taken in! It's two inches too long!"
>
> The tailor says, "No, just bend your elbow like this. See, it pulls up the sleeve."
>
> The man says, "Well, okay, but now look at the collar! When I bend my elbow, the collar goes halfway up the back of my head."
>
> The tailor says, "So? Raise your head up and back. Perfect."
>
> The man says, "But now the left shoulder is three inches lower than the right one!"
>
> The tailor says, "No problem. Bend at the waist way over to the left and it evens out."
>
> The man leaves the shop wearing the suit, his right elbow crooked and sticking out, his head up and back, all the while leaning down to the left. The only way he can walk is with a jerky, awkward gait.
>
> Just then, two passersby notice him.
>
> Says the first: "Look at that poor crippled guy. My heart goes out to him."
>
> Says the second: "Yeah, but his tailor must be a genius! That suit fits him perfectly!"

Synthetic versus analytic, right? (And we're not talking fabric here.) The stranger thinks, "This man's tailor fit him perfectly with a suit" is a synthetic *a posteriori* statement purporting to provide information, based on observation, about the tailor and his apparent skill in making the suit. But for the tailor,

"This suit I made is a perfect-fitting suit" is really an analytic statement. It is the same as saying, "This suit I made is a suit I made." That's because *any* suit the man tries on will be a perfect fit, as the tailor fits the man *to* the suit.

KANT'S CLOCK

Kant gave primacy to pure reason, so much so that he saw little need for personal experience in solving the problems of knowledge. Accordingly, he never ventured outside his hometown of Königsberg and lived a solitary life of extremely regular habits, like his daily, post-dinner walk. It is said that the citizens of Königsberg set their clocks according to the position of Professor Kant on this daily walk down and back the same street (which later became known as the *Philosophengang*, or "The Philosopher's Walk").

Less well known (possibly because it may not be true) is that the sexton of Königsberg Cathedral also confirmed the time on the church tower clock by observing when Kant took his daily promenade, *and Kant in turn scheduled his walk by the church tower clock.*

Talk about a confusion between analytic and synthetic! Both Kant and the sexton think they are gaining new information by observing the other's behaviour. Kant thinks that by observing the tower clock he is learning the official German standard time which, in turn, was established by observing the earth's rotation. The sexton thinks that by observing Kant's daily walk he is learning standard German time because of the sexton's belief in Kant's inherent punctuality. In fact, each was simply arriving at an analytic conclusion, true by definition. Kant's conclusion, "I take my walk at 3:30," really boils down to an analytic statement "I take my walk when I take my walk"—because how Kant determines it is 3:30 is by a clock that has been calibrated to his walk. The sexton's conclusion, "My clock is correct," boils down to "My clock says what my clock says"—because his criterion for the accuracy of his clock is Kant's walk, which was in turn based on what his clock says.

Philosophy of Mathematics

What about Dimitri's acute insight that $2 + 2 = 4$? Is that an analytic statement, true by definition? Is part of what we mean by "4" that it is the sum of 2 and 2? Or is it synthetic? Does it provide us with new knowledge about the world? Did we come to it by counting two things and then counting two more things and then counting the whole pile? The latter is the approach taken by the Voohoona tribe in the Australian outback.

A western anthropologist is told by a Voohooni that $2 + 2 = 5$. The anthropologist asks him how he knows this. The tribesman says, "By counting, of course. First I tie two knots in a cord. Then I tie two knots in another cord. When I join the two cords together, I have five knots."

Much of the philosophy of mathematics is quite technical and difficult. The only thing you really need to know is that, when it comes to mathematics, there are three kinds of people: those who can count and those who can't.

Pragmatism

For an epistemological pragmatist like the late-nineteenth-century American philosopher William James, the truth of a statement lies in its practical consequences. According to James, we *choose* our truth by what difference it will make in practice. We say Newton's law of gravity is true, not because it corresponds to the way things "really are," but because it has proven *useful* in predicting the behaviour of two objects relative to each other under many different sorts of circumstances: "Hey, I bet apples would fall down even in New Jersey." The day a theory stops being useful is the day we will replace it with some other one.

A woman reports her husband's disappearance to the police. They ask her for a description, and she says, "He's six feet, three inches tall, well-built, with thick, curly hair."

Her friend says, "What are you talking about? Your husband is five-feet-four, bald, and has a huge belly."

And she says, "Who wants that one back?"

This much of the story is well known. You may have heard it yourself. What is not so well known is the dialogue that followed:

The police say, "Lady, we are asking you for a description of your husband that corresponds to your actual husband."

The woman responds, "Correspondence, shmorrespondence! Truth cannot be determined solely by epistemological criteria, because the adequacy of those criteria cannot be determined apart from the goals sought and values held. That is to say, in the end, truth is what satisfies, and, God knows, my husband didn't do that."

Phenomenology

After flights to the height of abstraction, philosophy has a way of coming in for a soft landing in ordinary everyday experience. This happened in epistemology in the early twentieth century when the phenomenologists weighed in on what it really means to know something. More a methodology than a set of philosophical principles, phenomenology attempts to understand human experience as it is lived rather than as objective data. This approach is more like a novelist's than an abstraction-prone philosopher's.

The German word *einfühlung,* meaning "feeling into" or "empathy," was used by phenomenologists such as Edmund Husserl to refer to a mode of knowing that attempts to get inside the experience of another human being and to know and to feel the world in the same way he or she does; in other words, to put yourself in another person's shoes—or possibly pants.

"Dr. Janet," the embarrassed woman says, "I have a sexual problem. I don't get aroused by my husband."

Dr. Janet says, "Okay, I'll do a thorough exam tomorrow. Bring your husband in with you."

The next day the woman returns with her husband. "Take off your clothes, Mr. Thomas," says the doctor. "Now turn all the way around. Okay, now lie down, please. Uh-huh, I see. Okay, you may put your clothes back on."

Dr. Janet takes the woman aside. "You're in perfect health," she says. "He doesn't turn me on either."

DIMITRI: I've got to admit, Tasso, this epistemology stuff is good to know.

TASSO: Good? In what way? What do you mean by "good"?

DIMITRI: Before I answer that, I have a question for you. Do you know what "pain in the ass" means?

Ethics

Sorting out what's good and bad is the province of ethics. It is also what keeps priests, pundits, and parents busy. Unfortunately, what keeps children and philosophers busy is asking the priests, pundits, and parents, "Why?"

DIMITRI: I've been thinking about your question, what does "good" mean, and I've got the answer—"good" is acting on a just principle.

TASSO: By Zeus, Dimitri, you're full of surprises—you're starting to sound like a real philosopher. Just one last question: How do you determine just principles?

DIMITRI: Du-uh! Just like everybody else. I learn them from my mother.

TASSO (aside): Why does Socrates get all the "A" students?

Absolutist Ethics: Divine Law

Divine Law makes a simple business of ethics: If God says it's wrong, it *is* wrong, wholly and absolutely. That's all she wrote. But there are complications. The first is, how can we be sure what God really thinks? Fundamentalists have that one covered: Scripture says so. But how did the people in Scripture know the signals they were getting were really from God? Abraham thought he was called by God to sacrifice his son on the altar. Abraham figures, "If God says so, I'd better do it." Our first philosophical query to Abraham is, "What are you, nuts? You hear 'God' tell you to do a crazy thing, and you don't even ask for identification?"

Another problem with following Divine Law is interpretation. What exactly qualifies as honouring thy father and mother? A Mother's Day card? Marrying the boring son of the family dentist, as thy honourable mother and father want you to do? These questions don't feel like Talmudic hair-splitting when the dentist's son is 4' 11" and weighs twenty stone.

A prime characteristic of Divine Law is that God always has the last word.

A young and lusty St. Augustine apparently attempted a similar negotiation when he famously cried out, "Lord, grant me chastity. But not *now*!" Clearly, Augustine was trying a little Talmudic hair-splitting himself. "I mean, you didn't say exactly *when* not to commit adultery, did you?" Sounds like a joke.

Moses trudges down from Mt. Sinai, tablets in hand, and announces to the assembled multitudes: "I've got good news and I've got bad news. The good news is I got Him down to ten. The bad news is 'adultery' is still in."

Platonic Virtue

In his magnum opus, *The Republic*, Plato wrote, "The state is the soul writ large." So to discuss the virtues of the individual, he wrote a dialogue about the virtues of the ideal state. He called the rulers of this state Philosopher Kings, which may account for Plato's popularity with philosophers. The Philosopher Kings guide the state as Reason guides the human soul. The prime virtue—of both the PKs and Reason—is Wisdom, which Plato defined as understanding the Idea of the Good. However, one man's good is another man's goodies.

At a meeting of the university faculty, an angel suddenly appears and tells the head of the philosophy department, "I will grant you whichever of three blessings you choose: Wisdom, Beauty—or ten million dollars."

Immediately, the professor chooses Wisdom.

There is a flash of lightning, and the professor appears transformed, but he just sits there, staring down at the table. One of his colleagues whispers, "Say something."

The professor says, "I should have taken the money."

Stoicism

The ethical question that concerned the Stoics in the fourth century B.C. was how to react to the prevailing sense of fatalism that came from living in a tightly controlled empire. They could not change much of anything in their daily lives, so they decided to change their attitude toward life itself. It was the only personal control they had left. What the Stoics came up with was a strategy of emotional disengagement from life. They called their attitude *apathia* (apathy) and for the Stoics apathy was a virtue, which made them a barrel of laughs at the local taverna. The Stoics were willing to sacrifice some kinds of happiness (sex, drugs, and Dionysian hip-hop) in order to avoid the unhappiness brought on by their passions (STDs, hangovers, and bad rhymes). They acted only from reason, never from passion, and therefore considered themselves the only truly happy people—which is to say they were un-unhappy.

In the following story, Mr. Cooper demonstrates a modern form of Stoicism: Stoicism by proxy.

The Coopers were shown into the dentist's office, where Mr. Cooper made it clear he was in a big hurry. "No fancy stuff, Doctor," he ordered. "No gas or needles or any of that stuff. Just pull the tooth and get it over with."

"I wish more of my patients were as stoic as you," said the dentist admiringly. "Now, which tooth is it?"

Mr. Cooper turned to his wife. "Open your mouth, honey."

G. K. Chesterton once wrote, "The word 'good' has many meanings. For example, if a man were to shoot his mother at a range of five hundred yards, I should call him a good shot, but not necessarily a good man." It's the qualifier "necessarily" that shows Chesterton possessed a truly philosophical mind.

Utilitarianism

We all know that that twentieth-century pinko Vladimir Lenin said, "The end justifies the means," but, ironically, it's not too far from the view of one of the right wing's favorite philosophers, John Stuart Mill. Mill and the utilitarians proposed a "consequentialist" ethic: The moral rightness of an act is determined solely by its consequences.

The protagonist in the following story is clearly a utilitarian:

Mrs. O'Callahan instructed the artist painting her portrait to add to it a gold bracelet on each of her wrists, a strand of pearls around her neck, ruby earrings, and a diamond tiara.

The artist pointed out that would be tantamount to lying.

Said Mrs. O'Callahan, "Look, my husband's running around with a young blonde. After I die, I want her to go crazy looking for the jewellery."

This sort of justification could presumably be used to condone some pretty serious stuff, if the consequences were felt to be "good" enough.

Mrs. Brevoort, a widow, was hanging out by the pool at her country club when she spotted a handsome man sunning himself. She sidled up to him and said, "Well, I don't believe I've seen you here before."

"Not likely," the man said. "I've been in the penitentiary for thirty years."

"Really? What for?"

"I murdered my wife."

"Ah!" Mrs. Brevoort said, "So you're single!"

The influential contemporary utilitarian Peter Singer often draws analogies between decisions that we all agree involve horrendous consequences and more seemingly benign decisions that he contends are ethically similar. In one essay, he poses a situation in which one can earn money to buy a new TV by selling a homeless child to a corporation that will harvest his organs for transplants. Way bad, we all agree. But then Singer argues that any time one buys a new TV in lieu of sending money to a charity that protects homeless children, he is doing essentially the same thing. Don't you hate it when he says things like that? It's an argument by analogy from a dramatic particular to a general moral pronouncement, like in this classic gag:

He: Would you sleep with me for a million pounds?

She: A million quid? Wow! I guess I would.

He: How about for two dollars?

She: Get lost, mate! What do you think I am?

He: We've already established that. Now we're just haggling over the price.

The Supreme Categorical Imperative and the Olden Goldie

Kant's overarching principle, the criterion for all other ethical maxims, is what he calls the "supreme categorical imperative." At first, this imperative merely sounds like a dressed-up version of the old golden rule.

Golden rule:"Do unto others as you would have others do unto you."

Supreme categorical imperative: "Act only according to that maxim whereby you can at the same time will that it should become a universal law."

Of course, Kant's rendition has a decidedly colder ring to it. The very term "supreme categorical imperative" sounds, well, Germanic. But then Kant couldn't help it—he *was* German.

Still, the categorical imperative and the golden rule *do* share a lot of philosophical territory:

- Neither of them is a rule about specific action, like
  "Honour thy father and mother" or "Eat your spinach!"

- Instead, both provide an abstract principle for determining which specific actions are right and which are wrong.

- In both, this abstract principle invokes the idea that all people are as valuable as you and me, and so all should be treated morally the same as you and me . . . particularly me.

But there *is* a fundamental difference between the categorical imperative and the golden rule, and this one-liner hits it on the head:

A sadist is a masochist who follows the golden rule.

In inflicting pain on others, the masochist is only doing what the golden rule requires: doing what he would like done unto him, preferably with a whip. But Kant would say that there's no way the masochist could honestly claim that the moral imperative, "inflict pain on others," could be a universal law for a livable world. Even a masochist would find that unreasonable.

Similar considerations led English playwright George Bernard Shaw to wryly rewrite the golden rule:

"Do not do unto others as you would have others do unto you; they may have different taste."

Variations on the golden rule are found not only in Kant, but in religious traditions from around the world:

HINDUISM (c. THIRTEENTH CENTURY B.C.)
Do not to others what ye do not wish done to yourself . . .
This is the whole Dharma. Heed it well.
—*The Mahabharata*

JUDAISM (c. THIRTEENTH CENTURY B.C.)
What is hateful to you, do not do to your neighbour; that
is the entire Torah; the rest is commentary; go learn it.
—*The Babylonian Talmud*

ZOROASTRIANISM (c. TWELFTH CENTURY B.C.)
Human nature is good only when it does not do unto
another whatever is not good for its own self.
—*The Dadistan-i-Dinik*

BUDDHISM (c. SIXTH CENTURY B.C.)
Hurt not others in ways that you yourself would find
hurtful.
—The Tibetan *Dhammapada*

CONFUCIANISM (c. SIXTH CENTURY B.C.)
Do not do to others what you do not want done
to yourself.
—Confucius, *Analects*

ISLAM (c. seventh century a.d.)
No one of you is a believer until you desire for another
that which you desire for yourself.
—"The Sunnah," from *The Hadith*

BAHÁ'Í (c. nineteenth century a.d.)
Ascribe not to any soul that which thou wouldst not
have ascribed to thee, and say not that which thou doest
not. This is my command unto thee, do thou observe it.
—Bahá'u'lláh, *The Hidden Words*

SOPRANOISM (twenty-first century a.d.)
Whack the next guy with the same respect you'd like to
be whacked with, you know?
—Tony, Episode Twelve

Will to Power

The nineteenth-century German philosopher Friedrich Nietzsche boldly proclaimed that he was turning traditional Christian ethics on its ear. He started small, by announcing the death of God. God retaliated by announcing—on the walls of men's cubicles in university towns—the death of Nietzsche. What Nietzsche meant by the death of God was that Western culture had outgrown metaphysical explanations of the world as well as the accompanying Christian ethic. He called Christianity "herd morality," because it teaches an "unnatural ethic"—that it's bad to be an alpha male who dominates the herd. In place of Christian ethics he substituted a life-affirming ethic of strength, which he called the will to power. The exceptional individual, the *Übermensch* or superman, is above herd morality and deserves to express his natural strength and superiority freely over the herd. Friedrich was clearly a member of the Tony Soprano school when it came to the golden rule. Consequently, Nietzsche has been blamed for everything from German militarism to sauerkraut:

The problem with German food is that, no matter how much you eat, an hour later you're hungry for power.

Emotivism

By the mid-twentieth century, most ethical philosophy was metaethical. Instead of asking, "What actions are good?" philosophers were asking, "What does it *mean* to say an action is good? Does 'x is good' mean only 'I approve of x'? Alternatively, does 'x is good' express an emotion I feel when I observe x or think about x?" The latter stance, known as emotivism, finds expression in this story:

A man wrote a letter to the tax office saying, "I have been unable to sleep knowing that I have cheated on my income tax. I

have understated my taxable income and have enclosed a cheque
for £150. If I still can't sleep, I will send the rest."

Applied Ethics

Just when metaethical speculation about the meaning of the
word "good" was beginning to run out of steam, *doing* ethics
became fashionable again, and philosophers began to write
once more about what particular actions are good. Bioethics,
feminist ethics, and ethics for the proper treatment of animals
became de rigeur.

One type of applied ethics that burgeoned in the twentieth
century was professional ethics, the codes regulating the rela-
tionships of professionals to clients and patients.

After attending a conference on professional ethics, four
psychiatrists walked out together. One said, "You know, people
are always coming to us with their guilt and fears, but we
have no one to go to with our problems. So why don't we take
some time right now to hear each other out?" The other
three agreed.

The first psychiatrist confessed, "I have an almost
uncontrollable desire to kill my patients."

The second psychiatrist said, "I find ways to cheat my patients
out of their money whenever I can."

The third followed with, "I'm involved in selling drugs and often
get my patients to sell them for me."

The fourth psychiatrist then confessed, "You know, no matter how hard I try, I can't seem to keep a secret."

Each medical specialty developed its own ethical principles.

Four docs went on a duck-hunting trip together: a family practitioner, a gynaecologist, a surgeon, and a pathologist. As a bird flew overhead, the family practitioner started to shoot but decided not to because he wasn't absolutely sure it was a duck. The gynaecologist also started to shoot, but lowered his gun when he realized he didn't know whether it was a male or a female duck. The surgeon, meanwhile, blew the bird away, turned to the pathologist and said, "Go see if that was a duck."

Even lawyers have professional ethics. If a client mistakenly gives a lawyer £400 to pay a £300 bill, the ethical question that naturally arises is whether the lawyer should tell his partner.

It should come as no surprise that clergy also have professional ethics or that theirs come with divine sanctions.

The young rabbi was an avid golfer. Even on Yom Kippur, the holiest day of the year, he snuck out by himself for a quick nine holes.

On the last hole he teed off, and a gust of wind carried his ball directly over the hole and dropped it in for a hole in one.

An angel who witnessed this miracle complained to God, "This guy is playing golf on Yom Kippur, and you cause him to get a hole in one? This is a punishment?"

"Of course it is," said the Lord, smiling. "Who can he tell?"

What makes applied ethics interesting, but also puzzling, is that ethical decisions often turn on a dilemma, a tough choice between two goods: "How much allegiance do I owe my family as opposed to my job? My kids as opposed to myself? My country as opposed to humanity?" It's those practical ethical dilemmas that kept agony aunts in business all those years and now provide the material for "The Ethicist," Kwame Anthony Appiah's weekly column for *The New York Times*.

Appiah's precdecessor, Randy Cohen, revealed one of the best questions he's never been asked:

Although I'm happy in my current job, having recently received a promotion (I'm the new Thane of Cawdor), that's not enough for my wife who is eager for me to get ahead. I'm not saying I lack ambition, but I am reluctant to do what it takes to climb higher—the long hours, the bloody murders. And yet, don't I have a special obligation to consider my wife's desires? We are, after all, a family.

—MACBETH, SCOTLAND

The Impact of Psychoanalysis on Philosophical Ethics

Sigmund Freud, though not a philosopher, had a dramatic impact on ethical philosophy with his assertion that it is really unconscious biological drives that determine human behaviour, not nice, rational, philosophical distinctions. No matter how hard we try to bring our lives under rational control, as the moral philosophers would have us do, our unconscious is always breaking through. The Freudian slip, for example, occurs when we "mistakenly" say something that expresses our unconscious desires, as when the city councillor introduces his gorgeous chairwoman as "a great pubic servant."

A therapist asks his patient how his visit to his mother went. The patient says, "It did not go well at all. I made a terrible Freudian slip."

"Really?" says the therapist. "What did you say?"

"What I meant to say was, 'Please pass the salt.' But what I said was, 'You bitch! You ruined my life!'"

For Freud, all the ethical philosophy in the world tells us less about the true, unconscious controllers of our behaviour than one good dream.

A man comes rushing into his psychiatrist's office, apologizing for being late because he overslept.

"But I had an incredible breakthrough in my dream," the man says breathlessly. "I was talking with my mother and she suddenly turned into *you*! That's when I woke up, got dressed, grabbed a Coke and a donut, and rushed to your office."

The psychiatrist says: "A Coke and a donut? You call that a *breakfast?*"

On the other hand, even Freud admitted that reducing human behaviour to unconscious drives could sometimes miss the obvious truth. He famously said, "Sometimes a cigar is just a cigar."

A man is shaving with a straight-edged razor when the razor drops out of his hands and lops off his penis. He gathers it up, stuffs it in his pocket, rushes outside and hails a cab, telling the driver to get him to the emergency room fast.

There he tells the surgeon what happened and the surgeon says, "We'll have to work quickly. Give it to me."

The man reaches into his pocket and deposits its contents in the surgeon's hand.

"But this is a cigar," says the surgeon, "not a penis!"

And the man says, "Oh, my God, I must have smoked it in the cab."

Situation Ethics

In the 1960s came all the flap about "situation ethics." Proponents claimed that the ethical thing to do in any situation is dependent on the peculiar mix of factors in that situation. Who are the people affected? What legitimate stake do they have in the outcome? How will the outcome influence future situations? And who's asking anyhow? In a case of infidelity, for example, situation ethicists would want to know, among other things, about the status of the marriage. They might end up on different sides of the issue depending on whether the marriage was already effectively over. Opponents of situation ethics voiced their outrage, sensing that such reasoning might be used to justify anything a person wanted to do. Some of these opponents took an absolutist position: Infidelity is always wrong, regardless of the circumstances.

Paradoxically, however, it is sometimes by *ignoring* the specifics of the situation that we create the opportunity for self-serving action.

Armed robbers burst into a bank, line up customers and staff against the wall, and begin to take their wallets, watches, and jewellery. Two of the bank's accountants are among those waiting to be robbed. The first accountant suddenly thrusts something in the hand of the other. The second accountant whispers, "What is this?" The first accountant whispers back, "It's the fifty bucks I owe you."

DIMITRI: I'm still not sure what's right and what's wrong, but one thing's for sure—the important thing in life is to make the gods happy.

TASSO: Like Zeus and Apollo.

DIMITRI: Right. Or my personal favourite, Aphrodite.

TASSO: One of my favourites too . . . if she exists.

DIMITRI: If she exists? You better watch your mouth, Tasso. I've seen grown men get whammed by a thunderbolt for talking like that.

Philosophy of Religion

The God that philosophers of religion like to argue about isn't one that most of us would recognize. He tends to be more on the abstract side, like "The Force" in Star Wars, *and less like a Heavenly Father who stays up at night worrying about you.*

DIMITRI: I was talking to Zeus the other day, and he thinks you're a bad influence on me.

TASSO: That's interesting, because I think he's a bad influence on you.

DIMITRI: In what way?

TASSO: He makes you think the voices in your head are real.

Belief in God

An agnostic is a person who thinks that God's existence cannot be proven on the basis of current evidence, but who doesn't deny the possibility that God exists. The agnostic is one step short of an atheist, who considers the case against the existence of God closed. If both of them came across a burning bush saying, "I am that I am," the agnostic would start looking for the hidden tape recorder, but the atheist would just shrug and reach for his marshmallows.

So these two Irish drinking buddies are in the pub when they see a bald guy drinking alone at the end of the bar.

Pat: I say, ain't that Winnie Churchill down there?

Sean: Nah. Couldn't be. Winnie wouldn't be in a place like this.

Pat: I'm not kidding. Take a good look. I swear that's Winnie Churchill. I'll bet you ten quid I'm right.

Sean: You're on!

So Pat goes down to the end of the bar and says to the bald guy, "You're Winnie Churchill, ain't ya?"

And Bald Guy screams, "Get out of my face, you idiot!"

Pat comes back to Sean and says, "Guess we'll never know now, will we?"

Now that's thinking like an agnostic.

Atheists are another story. Philosophers agreed long ago that it is fruitless for believers and atheists to argue with each other. This is because they interpret *everything* differently. In order to argue, there must be some common ground, so that one of the participants can say, "Aha! If you concede x, then you must also concede y!" Atheists and believers never find an x they can agree upon. The argument can never begin, because each sees *everything* from his own point of view. That's a little abstract, but this story brings it down to earth—in fact, right into the neighbourhood.

A little old Christian lady comes out onto her front porch every morning and shouts, "Praise the Lord!"

And every morning the atheist next door yells back, "There is no God!"

This goes on for weeks. "Praise the Lord!" yells the lady. "There is no God!" responds the neighbour.

As time goes by, the lady runs into financial difficulties and has trouble buying food. She goes out onto the porch and asks God for help with groceries, then says, "Praise the Lord!"

The next morning when she goes out onto the porch, there are the groceries she asked for. Of course, she shouts, "Praise the Lord!"

The atheist jumps out from behind a bush and says, "Ha! I bought those groceries. There is no God!"

The lady looks at him and smiles. She shouts, "Praise the Lord! Not only did you provide for me, Lord, you made Satan pay for the groceries!"

Sam Harris, in his 2005 bestselling book, *The End of Faith*, provides what could be a stand-up routine based on his observations of religious faith:

"Tell a devout Christian his wife is cheating on him, or that frozen yoghurt can make a man invisible, and he is likely to require as much evidence as anybody else, and to be persuaded only to the extent that you give it. Tell him that the book he keeps by his bed was written by an invisible deity who will punish him with fire for eternity if he fails to accept its every incredible claim, and he seems to require no evidence whatsoever."

Harris fails to mention the downside of being an atheist—you have nobody to cry out to in the throes of an orgasm.

The seventeenth-century French mathematician and philosopher Blaise Pascal argued that deciding whether or not to believe in God is essentially engaging in a wager. If we choose to behave as if there is a God and we get to the end and it turns out there isn't, it's not such a big deal. Well, maybe we've lost the ability to thoroughly enjoy the Seven Deadly Sins, but that's small potatoes compared to the alternative. If we bet there isn't a God, and get to the end only to find out there is a God, we've lost the Big Enchilada, eternal bliss. Therefore, according to Pascal, it is a better strategy to live as if there is a God. This is known to academics as "Pascal's wager." To the rest of us, it's known as hedging your bets.

Inspired by Pascal's *Pensées*, a little old lady goes to the bank with a satchel filled with £100,000 in cash and asks to open an account. The cautious banker asks where she got the money. "Gambling," she says. "I'm very good at gambling."

Intrigued, the banker asks, "What sorts of bets do you make?"

"Oh, all sorts," she says. "For example, I will bet you £25,000 right now that by noon tomorrow you will have a butterfly tattoo on your right buttock."

"Well, I would love to take that bet," says the banker, "but it wouldn't be right for me to take your money for such an absurd wager."

"Let me put it to you this way," says the woman. "If you don't bet me, I'll have to find another bank for my money."

"Now, now, don't be hasty," says the banker. "I'll take your bet."

The woman returns the next day at noon with her lawyer as a witness. The banker turns around, drops his pants, and invites the two to observe that he has won the bet. "Okay," says the woman, "but could you bend over a little just to make sure?" The banker obliges and the woman concedes, counting out £25,000 in cash from her satchel.

The lawyer meanwhile is sitting with his head in his hands. "What's wrong with him?" asks the banker.

"Aw, he's just a sore loser," she says. "I bet him £100,000 that by noon today, you'd moon us in your office."

There's a fine line between hedging a bet and rigging the odds. Consider this neo-Pascalian strategy:

A man with a parrot on his shoulder attends services on the first day of Rosh Hashanah. He bets several people that the parrot can lead the service more beautifully than the cantor. When the time comes, though, the parrot is totally silent. At home afterward, the man berates the parrot and bemoans his losses. The parrot says, "Use your head, schmuck! Think of the odds we can get now on Yom Kippur!"

Hey, maybe this parrot is on to something. Maybe we can

rig the odds of Pascal's wager so that we can play golf on Sunday morning and still keep God happy, if he happens to exist! God knows we've all tried.

Deism and Historical Religion

Eighteenth-century philosophers, if they weren't skeptics, tended to be Deists, believers in a remote, impersonal God-of-the-philosophers—a Creator more like a force than a person, more like a clockmaker than a confidant. Traditional Jews and Christians pushed back. Their God, they said, was no mere clockmaker. He was the Lord of history, present in the Exodus from Egypt, the wandering in the desert, and the settling of the Promised Land. He was, in a word, available—a "very present help in trouble."

A Jewish grandmother is watching her grandchild playing on the beach when a huge wave comes and takes him out to sea. She pleads, "Please God, save my only grandson. I beg of you, bring him back."

And a big wave comes and washes the boy back onto the beach, good as new.

She looks up to heaven and says: "He had a hat!"

Try saying that to a clockmaker!

"Then, each month, you'll receive a new set of commandments.
Cancel anytime and keep the first set, absolutely free."

Theological Distinctions

While philosophers of religion are worrying about Big Questions—like, "Is there a God?"—theologians have smaller fish to fry, usually during Lent.

According to twentieth-century philosopher *and* theologian Paul Tillich, there's more to the difference between the philosophy of religion and theology than the size of their fish. The philosopher, he says, pursues truth about God and God-stuff as objectively as possible, while the theologian is *already* "grasped by faith" and engaged and committed. In other words, the philosopher of religion looks at God and religion from the outside, while the theologian looks at them from the inside.

In theology, schisms have opened over such pressing issues as, "Does the Spirit proceed from the Father or from the Father *and* the Son?" The layperson clearly needs a simple guide to theological differences and, thank God, the comedians are always willing to oblige. The key to determining the religious persuasion of a person, it turns out, is whom he does or does not recognize:

Jews don't recognize Jesus.

Protestants don't recognize the Pope.
Baptists don't recognize each other in the off license.

This last point translates into some very practical advice. If you're going fishing, don't invite a Baptist; he'll drink all the beer. However, if you invite two Baptists, you'll have it all to yourself.

Another way to differentiate denominations is according to what behaviour qualifies someone for a divine dressing-down. For Catholics, it's missing Mass. For Baptists, it's dancing. For Episcopalians, it's eating your salad with your dessert fork.

But seriously, folks, there are important doctrinal differences among the denominations. For example, Catholics alone believe in the Immaculate Conception, the doctrine that in order to be able to carry the Lord, Mary herself was born without the taint of Original Sin.

Jesus was walking through the streets when he noticed a crowd of people throwing stones at an adulteress. Jesus said, "Let whoever is without sin cast the first stone." Suddenly a rock flew through the air. Jesus turned and said, "Mother?"

Everyone's favorite sub-genre of sectarianism jokes, of course, is the Counter-Reformation joke. Your basic collection of great Counter-Reformation jokes always contains this one:

A man is in desperate financial straits and prays to God to save him by letting him win the lottery.

Days go by, then weeks, and the man fails to win a single lottery. Finally, in misery, he cries out to God, "You tell us, 'Knock and it shall be opened to you. Seek and you shall find.' I'm going down the tubes here, and I still haven't won the lottery!"

A voice from above answers, "You've got to meet me half way, bubbeleh! Buy a ticket!"

This man was clearly a Protestant, who, like Martin Luther, thought that we are saved by grace alone; there is nothing we can do to earn salvation. God, on the other hand, despite his apt use of the word "bubbeleh," is here carrying water for the Catholic Counter-Reformation. In fact, this joke may well have originated at the Council of Trent in 1545, where the bishops decided that salvation comes via a combination of grace *and* works, prayer *and* buying a ticket.

One belief that all the denominations have in common is that only their own theology is the fast track to the divine.

A man arrives at the gates of heaven. St. Peter asks, "Religion?"

The man says, "Methodist." St. Peter looks down his list, and says, "Go to room twenty-eight, but be very quiet as you pass room eight."

Another man arrives at the gates of heaven. "Religion?" "Baptist."

"Go to room eighteen, but be very quiet as you pass room eight."

A third man arrives at the gates. "Religion?"

"Jewish."

"Go to room eleven, but be very quiet as you pass room eight."

The man says, "I can understand there being different rooms for different religions, but why must I be quiet when I pass room eight?"

St. Peter says, "The Jehovah's Witnesses are in room eight, and they think they're the only ones here."

It has been said that the nineteenth-century German philosopher Arthur Schopenhauer discovered Buddhism philosophically. Like Gautama the Buddha two millennia earlier, Schopenhauer thought that all life is suffering, struggle, and frustration, and the only escape is resignation—the rejection of desire and denial of the will to live. On the upside, they both thought that resignation would lead to compassion for all beings and saintliness. Like, it's a tradeoff.

A number of Jewish jokes poke fun at the ultimate Schopenhaueresque pessimist, the *kvetcher* (griper).

Two women are sitting on a bench. After a while the first woman says, "Oy!"

The second woman replies, "Oy!"

The first woman says, "All right, enough about the children."

For both Arthur Schopenhauer and the Buddha, life is a constant cycle of frustration and boredom. When we don't have what we want, we're frustrated. When we do have what we want, we're bored. And for both Artie and Gautama, the worst frustration occurs just when relief appears to be within one's grasp.

Once upon a time there was a prince who, through no fault of his own, was placed under a spell by an evil witch. The curse was that the prince could speak only one word each year. He could, however, save up credits, so if he did not speak at all in one year, he could speak two words the following year.

One day he met a beautiful princess and fell madly in love. He decided to refrain from speaking for two years so that he could look at her and say, "My darling."

At the end of the two years, however, he wanted to also tell her he loved her, so he decided to wait three more years, for a total of five years of silence. At the end of the five years, though, he knew he had to ask her to marry him, so he needed to wait still another four years.

Finally, as his ninth year of silence ended, he was understandably overjoyed. He led the princess to the most romantic part of the royal garden, knelt before her, and said, "My darling, I love you. Will you marry me?"

The princess replied, "Pardon?"

It's just the kind of response Schopenhauer would have expected.

Starting in the sixth and seventh centuries A.D., the Chinese and Japanese developed a branch of Buddhism that is experiencing a renaissance today—Zen. From the perspective of Western thought, Zen philosophy is a kind of anti-philosophy. For the Zen master, reason, logic, sense data—all the stuff that Western philosophy is built upon—are illusions and distractions from ultimate enlightenment. So how does one become enlightened?

Consider the following two questions:

- What is the difference between a duck?
- What is the sound of one hand clapping?

Both questions elicit what is known in philosophical circles as a "Whaaa?" response. They don't scan. We just can't comprehend what an answer could possibly be. But while the first is a quaint bit of schoolyard nonsense, the second is a classic Zen *koan* (rhymes with Ben Cohen).

A *koan* is a riddle or story that, when told by a Zen master to a student, has the possibility of shocking that student into a state of consciousness known as *satori*—sudden enlightenment. In this consciousness, all the distinctions and evaluations of the everyday world evaporate, leaving one with a profound appreciation of the unity of the universe and of all experience in the universe. A Zen response to the one-hand-clapping riddle is not something literal and scientific like, "The soft murmur of air being wafted by a moving, flat surface." No, the Zen response is more like, "Wow!" *Koans* catapult us to enlightenment by confounding our minds with impossible ideas. Get beyond those and, bang, you're in *satori*.

Everybody's favorite *koan* is:

> Before I sought enlightenment, the mountains were mountains and the rivers were rivers.
> While I sought enlightenment, the mountains were not mountains and the rivers were not rivers.
> After I reached *satori*, the mountains were mountains and the rivers were rivers.

We Westerners can get the general idea that enlightenment is not a matter of attaining some far-out consciousness. What we have trouble getting—and what constitutes the *koan*ic core of the mountain thing—is how enlightened consciousness can be both ordinary and transcendent simultaneously. You either have a feel for this kind of thing or you don't, and most of us in the West don't.

This raises the question of whether the old difference-between-a-duck riddle could be considered a sort of Western *koan*. After all, it rests on illogic and absurdity; it confounds reason. But judging by the responses to this riddle—the acid test when it comes to *koans*—the answer has to be no. A smile, maybe even a giggle, but no *satori* we've heard of.

Alas, it may be a cultural problem—most of us in the West simply cannot get our minds around the Eastern notion that if you cannot get your mind around something, you're on your way to enlightenment. Which leaves us with this lame, Western pseudo *koan*:

> If you have some ice cream, I will give it to you.
> If you have no ice cream, I will take it away from you.
> That's an ice cream *koan*.

> The most memorable *koans* have become part of Zen lore, handed down from generation to generation. For example, Hui-neng, the seventh-century Sixth Patriarch of Zen, famously asked, "What did your original face look like before you were born?" Los Angeles Lakers coach Phil Jackson, nicknamed "the Zenmeister," contributed, "If you meet the Buddha in the lane, feed him the ball."

Airhead Philosophy

Airhead philosophy appeared on the scene in the late 1960s, coincidentally with Harvard professor Timothy Leary's pronouncement that the way to enlightenment was through ingesting magic mushrooms. Subsequently dubbed "New Age Philosophy," airheadism is an amalgam of ancient Eastern philosophies and some medieval beliefs such as astrology, Tarot cards, and the kabbalah. "Affirmations"—statements such as, "I am at one with my duality" or, "As I learn to trust the Process, I no longer need to carry a gun"—are also an important part of New Age philosophy. This reminds us of the elderly woman who approached British poet Samuel Taylor Coleridge after a lecture in the early 1800s and said, "Mr. Coleridge, I've accepted the universe!!" Coleridge peered over the top of his glasses and said, "My God, madam, you'd better!"

Happily, we have jokemeisters to illuminate the dimness of New Age thought.

How many New Agers does it take to change a lightbulb?
None, they just start a "Coping with Darkness" support group.

If there's anything up-to-date about New Agers, it may be their belief in extraterrestrial beings that not only visit us, but invite us into their airships for dinner and romance. It takes a satirist to push the limits of such New Age beliefs to their logical extreme.

A Martian makes an emergency landing in Brooklyn and finds that a key part of his saucer has been damaged—the all-important *troover.* He goes into a deli and asks the counter man if he knows where he can find a *troover.* The man asks, "What's it look like?"

The Martian says, "It's round, kind of hard on the outside, soft on the inside, with a little hole in the middle."

The deli man says, "That sounds like a bagel. Here, does this look like what you need?"

The Martian says, "It's perfect! What do you use those for here?"

The deli man says, "Well, you'll probably find this hard to believe, but we eat them."

The Martian says, "You're kidding! You eat *troovers*?"

The deli guy says, "Yeah, here, try one."

The Martian is pretty skeptical, but he takes a bite. "Hey," he says, "with a little cream cheese, this wouldn't be half bad."

Another element in the New Agers' kit bag is their fascination with parapsychic phenomena, such as clairvoyance. Many Old Agers—aka rational thinkers—continue to believe that there is always a reasonable explanation for such phenomena.

"My grandfather knew the exact time of the exact day of the exact year that he would die."

"Wow, what an evolved soul! How did it come to him?"

"The judge told him."

Hea-vy!

DIMITRI: I still have one question: If Zeus doesn't exist, is Poseidon still his brother?

TASSO: You know, Dimitri, either you are one enlightened Buddhist, or you're a few bricks short of an amphitheater.

Existentialism

"Existence precedes essence." If you agree with that statement, you are an existentialist. If not, you still exist, but you're essentially out of it.

DIMITRI: I have to admit, Tasso, sometimes I wish I were more like you.

TASSO: But you can be! Existentially speaking, you are a totally self-originated being! You are who you create!

DIMITRI: That's terrific! Because I always wanted to be as tall as you.

To get our heads into existentialism, we need to understand nineteenth-century Hegelian Absolutism, the philosophical POV that the only true picture of life is from the outside looking in. Was it Rodney Dangerfield who said, "Much of the best comedy can be found in the tension between the Hegelian Absolute and man's existential estrangement?" Probably not. But if he had, the following classic joke is probably what Rodney would have meant.

A man is making love to his best friend's wife when they hear the husband's car in the driveway. He dives into the closet. The husband comes in, goes to the closet to hang up his jacket, sees his friend standing there naked, and says, "Lenny, what are *you* doing here?"

Lenny sheepishly shrugs and says, "Everybody's gotta be somewhere."

That's a Hegelian answer to an existentialist question. The husband wants to know why Lenny of all people is in this particular existential situation—naked and in his closet! But his putative friend, Lenny, for reasons of his own, chooses to answer a different question: "Why is anybody anywhere rather than nowhere?"—a question that only makes sense if you're a lofty German philosopher like Hegel.

Georg Wilhelm Friedrich Hegel maintained that history is the unfolding in time of "Absolute Spirit." The spirit of one age (say, uptight 1950s conformism) generates its own antithesis (the hippie movement of the 1960s), and the clash of the two creates a new synthesis (the "plastic hippies" of the 1970s, like Wall Street bankers with Beatles haircuts).

And so it goes, on and on, a *dialectic* of thesis / antithesis / synthesis (which becomes the new thesis) and so on.

Hegel thought he had jumped outside history and was looking down on "It All" from a transcendent point of view. He called this point of view the Absolute. And from up there things looked pretty okay. Wars? Just a move in the dialectic.

Pestilence? Just another move. Anxiety? Not to worry. The dialectic is on the move, and there's nothing to be done about it. Just hang on and take in the scenery. Georg Wilhelm Friedrich thought he was looking at history from God's point of view!

Consider Bette Midler's golden oldie "From a Distance," in which the Divine Miss M imagines looking at the world from on high and finds the whole deal harmonious and groovy. That's the distance that Hegel is looking from. The song ends with none other than God looking over Bette's shoulder taking in the grand view. Who would have guessed Bette Midler is a Hegelian?

Enter Hegel's contemporary Søren Kierkegaard, and is he ever pissed off. "What difference does it make that all is well from the point of view of the Absolute?" Søren asks. That is not—and cannot be—the point of view of *existing individuals*. In that statement, existentialism was born. "*I* am not God," Søren said. "I am an individual. Who cares how peaceful it all is from on high? I'm right here in the finite thick of it and *I'm* anxious. *I'm* in danger of despair. *Me.* And so what if the universe is ineluctably rolling on—it's threatening to roll over *me*!"

So, if Kierkegaard finds you in his closet and asks, "What

are you doing here?" don't say, "Everybody's got to be some-where." Our advice: Improvise.

The twentieth-century French philosopher Jean-Paul Sartre picked up on Kierkegaard's idea of an individual's scary iso-lation and spun out the implications for human freedom and responsibility. The way Jean-Paul put it is, "existence precedes essence," by which he meant that human beings have no pre-determined essence the way, say, a coat-hanger does. We are indeterminate, always free to reinvent ourselves.

Jean-Paul Sartre was wall-eyed and altogether not a very handsome fellow. Therefore, he may have been taken aback when his fellow existentialist, Albert Camus, expanded Sartre's notion of human freedom by saying, "Alas, after a certain age every man is responsible for the face he has." Curiously, Camus looked a lot like Humphrey Bogart.

If we see ourselves as only objects with fixed identities, we cease to Be, with a capital B. And one way we see ourselves as objects is by identifying with a social role. That, Sartre says, is *mauvaise foi*, or bad faith. And that ain't good.

Sartre watches the waiter in the café and observes that to be a waiter is to *pretend* to be a waiter. Waiters learn how to become waiters by doing their impression of a waiter. Waiters walk a certain way, strike a certain attitude, stake out some point on the scale of intimacy versus distance, etc. This is fine as long as the waiter is conscious that it's only a role. But we all know waiters who believe they truly *are* waiters, that that is who they essentially are. *Très mauvaise foi!*

Jokes make fun of our tendency to unthinkingly identify with the attitudes and values of our social group by showing us exaggerated instances. This is itself a philosophical gambit: the *reductio ad absurdum*.

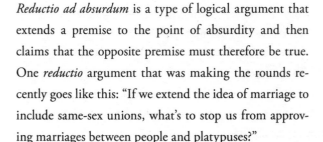

Reductio ad absurdum is a type of logical argument that extends a premise to the point of absurdity and then claims that the opposite premise must therefore be true. One *reductio* argument that was making the rounds recently goes like this: "If we extend the idea of marriage to include same-sex unions, what's to stop us from approving marriages between people and platypuses?"

In the following *reductio* joke, Sol gives new meaning to the bad faith inherent in identifying with a group.

Abe and his friend Sol are out for a walk. They pass a Catholic church with a sign out front that reads "£1,000 to Anyone Who

Converts." Sol decides to go inside and see what it's all about.
Abe waits outside. Hours go by. Finally, Sol emerges.

"So?" says Abe. "What happened?"

"I converted," says Sol.

"No kidding!" says Abe. "Did you get the thousand pounds?"

Sol says, "Is that all you people think about?"

(So we're not politically correct. We're philosophers. So sue
us!)

On the other hand, it is also bad faith to envision ourselves
as having unlimited possibilities with *no* constraints on our
freedom.

Two cows are standing in a field. One says to the other, "What
do you think about this mad cow disease?"

"What do I care?" says the other. "I'm a helicopter."

For the existentialist philosophers, *genuine* anxiety—the
one they call "angst" because it has such a bitter taste when
you say it—is not a symptom of pathology to be addressed by
therapy. No, it is a basic human response to the very conditions
of human existence: our mortality, our inability to fully realize
our potential, and the threat of meaninglessness. It's enough to
make you wish you were an airhead philosopher instead of an
existentialist.

The existentialists are eager to differentiate between "existential anxiety," such as the anxiety of death, which they feel

stems from the human condition, and ordinary neurotic anxiety, such as the anxiety of Norman:

Norman began to hyperventilate when he saw the doctor. "I'm sure I've got liver disease."

"That's ridiculous," said the doctor. "You'd never know if you had liver disease. There's no discomfort of any kind."

"Exactly!" said Norman. "Those are my precise symptoms."

The twentieth-century German existentialist Martin Heidegger would respond, You call that anxiety, Norman? You haven't lived yet. And by "lived" I mean thinking about death all the time! Heidegger went so far as to say that human existence is *being-toward-death*. To live authentically, we must face the fact of our own mortality squarely and take responsibility for living meaningful lives in the shadow of death. We must not try to escape personal anxiety and personal responsibility by denying the fact of death.

Three friends are killed in a car accident and meet up at an orientation session in Heaven. The celestial facilitator asks them what they would most like to hear said about themselves as their friends and relatives view them in the casket.

The first man says, "I hope people will say that I was a wonderful doctor and a good family man."

The second man says, "I would like to hear people say that as a schoolteacher I made a big difference in the lives of kids."

The third man says, "I'd like to hear someone say, 'Look, he's moving!'"

For Heidegger, it's not just that living in the shadow of death is more courageous; it's the only authentic way to live, because our number could come up any minute.

A man asks a fortuneteller what Heaven is like. The fortuneteller gazes into her crystal ball, and says, "Hmm, I see some good news and some bad news. The good news is that there are several golf courses in heaven and they are all incredibly beautiful."

"Wow! Terrific! What's the bad news?"

"You have an 8:30 tee time tomorrow morning."

Still in denial? Try this one:

Painter: How am I selling?

Gallery owner: Well, there's good news and bad news. A man came in and asked me if you were a painter whose work would become more valuable after your death. When I told him I thought you were, he bought everything you had in the gallery.

Painter: Wow! That's terrific! What's the bad news?

Gallery owner: He was your doctor.

However, every once in a while we hear a story about death that dares to look the ultimate angst right in the face and laugh at it. The American comedian Gilda Radner had the strength to tell this one in front of a live audience after she was diagnosed with terminal cancer.

A woman with cancer sees her oncologist, who says, "Well, I'm afraid we're finally at the end of the line. You only have eight hours to live. Go home and make the best of it."

The woman goes home, gives the news to her husband, and says, "Honey, let's just make love to each other all night long."

And the husband says, "You know how sometimes you're in the mood for sex and sometimes you aren't? Well, I'm just not in the mood tonight."

"Please," his wife pleads. "It's my final wish, darling."

"Just don't feel like it," the husband says.

"I beg you, darling!"

"Look," the husband says, "It's easy for you to say. You don't have to get up in the morning."

The existentialists' emphasis on facing the anxiety of death has given life to a new mini-industry, the hospice movement, founded on Dr. Elisabeth Kübler-Ross's twentieth-century bio-ethical philosophy that encourages the honest acceptance of death.

Customer in a restaurant: How do you prepare your chickens?

Cook: Oh, nothing special really. We just tell them they're gonna die.

TASSO: What are you laughing at? I'm talking about the angst of death here. It's no laughing matter.

DIMITRI: But there are worse things than death.

TASSO: Worse than death? Like what?

DIMITRI: Have you ever spent an entire evening with Pythagoras?

Philosophy of Language

When former president William Jefferson Clinton responded to a query, "It depends on what your definition of 'is' is," he was doing Language Philosophy. He may also have been doing other things.

DIMITRI: I'm finally beginning to see through you, Tasso. This whole philosophy business is just playing games with words!

TASSO: Exactly! Now we're getting somewhere.

DIMITRI: So you admit it! Philosophy is just semantics!

TASSO: *Just* semantics? How else could you do philosophy—with grunts and giggles?

Ordinary Language Philosophy

Ludwig Wittgenstein and his followers at Oxford University in the mid-twentieth century claimed that the classical philosophical questions—free will, the existence of God, and so forth—were puzzling only because they were posed in confused and confusing language. Their job as philosophers was to un-tangle linguistic knots, reframe questions, and do the next best thing to resolving the puzzles: make them go away.

For example, Descartes, back in the seventeenth century, had declared that people are composed of a mind and a body—with the mind being like a ghost in a machine. Philosophers then puzzled for centuries over what sort of thing this ghost is. Wittgenstein's Oxford disciple Gilbert Ryle said in effect, "Wrong question! It's not any sort of thing, because it isn't a thing at all. If we just look at the way we actually speak about so-called mental events, we can see that our words are really just a shorthand for describing behaviour. Nothing whatever is lost if we simply throw away the word for the 'place' behaviour supposedly comes from." Consider it disposed of, Gilly.

The young couple in the following story clearly needs to reframe their question:

A young married couple moves into a new apartment and decides to repaper the dining room. They call on a neighbour who has a dining room the same size and ask, "How many rolls of wallpaper did you buy when you papered your dining room?"

"Seven," he says.

So the couple buys seven rolls of expensive paper, and they start papering. When they get to the end of the fourth roll, the dining room is finished. Annoyed, they go back to the neighbour and say, "We followed your advice, but we ended up with three extra rolls!"

"So," he says, "that happened to you too."

Oops!

∽

As the poet Gertrude Stein lay on her deathbed, her partner, Alice B. Toklas, leaned over and whispered, "What is
the answer, Gertrude?"

Replied Stein, "What's the question?"

Wittgenstein blamed all the errors of Western philosophy on
what he termed "being bewitched by language," by which he
meant that words can trick us into miscategorizing things. We
are hoodwinked by the grammatical form of the sentences in
which philosophical questions are posed. For example, in his
magnum opus, *Being and Time,* Heidegger discussed "nothing"
as if it designated some weird *thing.* Here's a similar example of
linguistic confusion:

"Freddy, I hope you live to be a hundred, plus about three
months."

"Thank you, Alex. But why the three months?"

"I wouldn't want you to die suddenly."

If you think Alex is bewitched by language, consider
Garwood in the following story:

Garwood goes to a psychiatrist, where he complains he can never get a girlfriend.

"No wonder!" the shrink says. "You smell awful!"

"You said it," Garwood replies. "That's because of my job—I work in the circus following the elephants around and cleaning up their droppings. No matter how much I wash, the stink sticks to me."

"So quit your job and get another one!" the psychiatrist says.

"Are you crazy?" Garwood retorts. "And get out of show business?"

Garwood has confused the denotation of "show business," which, in his case, includes cleaning up after elephants, with the emotional connotation of "show business," in which being under the spotlight is all that matters.

According to the ordinary language philosophers, language has more than one purpose and is used differently in different contexts. Oxford philosopher John Austin pointed out that saying, "I promise," is a whole different linguistic deal from saying, "I paint." Saying, "I paint," is not the same thing as painting, but saying, "I promise," *is* the same thing as promising. Using language that is appropriate in one linguistic framework in a different linguistic framework is what causes philosophical confusions and pseudo puzzles, also known as the history of philosophy.

The ordinary language philosophers thought that the centuries-old philosophical struggle over belief in God grew out of trying to frame the question as one of fact. They said religious language is a different language altogether. Some said it is an evaluative language like the kind film critics Ebert and Roeper use: "I believe in God" really only means "I believe certain values get two thumbs way up." Others said religious language expresses emotions: "I believe in God" means, "When I ponder the universe, I get goosebumps!" Neither of these alternative languages results in the philosophical muddles you get by saying, "I believe in God." Poof! Puzzle resolved! And 2,500 years of the philosophy of religion down the tubes.

In the following story, Goldfinger and Fallaux are talking in two different linguistic contexts. It doesn't help that they speak two different languages.

Goldfinger is taking an ocean cruise. The first night he is seated for dinner with M. Fallaux, a Frenchman, who raises his glass to Goldfinger and says, "Bon appetit!"

Goldfinger raises his glass and replies, "Goldfinger!"

This goes on, meal after meal, for almost the entire voyage, but finally the ship's purser can't stand it any longer and explains to Goldfinger that "Bon appetit" is French for "Enjoy your meal."

Goldfinger is embarrassed and can't wait until the next meal to redeem himself. Then, before Fallaux can say anything, Goldfinger raises his glass and says, "Bon appetit!"

And Fallaux responds, "Goldfinger!"

Stories, in which the characters have different agendas,

provide goofy analogies to how differing linguistic frameworks muddle communication.

Tommy goes to confession and tells the priest, "Bless me, Father, for I have sinned. I have been with a loose woman."

"Is that you, Tommy?" says the priest.

"Aye, it is, Father."

"Who is it you were with, Tommy?"

"I'd rather not say, Father."

"Was it Bridget?"

"No, Father."

"Was it Colleen?"

"No, Father."

"Was it Megan?"

"No, Father."

"Well, Tommy, say four Our Fathers and four Hail Marys."

When Tommy gets outside, his friend Pat asks him how it went.

"Terrific," says Tommy. "I got four Our Fathers, four Hail Marys, and three great leads!"

In the following story, the priest is locked into his own understanding of the framework of the exchange he is having in the confessional and is unable to see the possibility of another.

A man goes into the confession booth and tells the priest, "Father, I'm seventy-five years old and last night I made love to two twenty-year-old girls—at the same time."

The priest says, "When did you last go to confession?"

The man says, "I've never been to confession, Father. I'm Jewish."

The priest says, "Then why are you telling me?"

The man says, "I'm telling everybody!"

A great number of jokes out there rest on *double entendres*, in which a phrase has a radically different significance when placed in a different linguistic framework. In fact, it is the *frisson* between the two frameworks that produces the chuckle.

In a bar is a piano player with a monkey that goes around after each number collecting tips. While the piano player is playing, the monkey jumps up on the bar, walks up to a customer, and squats over his drink, putting his testicles in the drink. The man is miffed, walks up to the piano player, and says, "Do you know your monkey dipped his balls in my martini?"

The piano player says, "No, man, but hum a few bars, and I can probably pick it up."

Many riddles try to trap us into assuming we are inside one linguistic frame, when in fact we are inside a very different one.

"Which of the following does not belong in this list: herpes, gonorrhoea, or a condominium in Cleveland?"

"The condo, obviously."

"Nope, gonorrhoea. It's the only one you can get rid of."

Ordinary language philosophy has been criticized as mere

wordplay, but Wittgenstein insisted that confusion of linguistic frameworks can lead to fatal mistakes.

Billingsley went to see his friend, Hatfield, who was dying in the hospital. As Billingsley stood by the bed, Hatfield's frail condition grew worse, and he gestured frantically for something to write on. Billingsley handed him a pen and a piece of paper, and Hatfield used his last ounce of strength to scribble a note. No sooner had he finished the note than he died. Billingsley put the note in his pocket, unable in his grief to read it just then.

A few days later as Billingsley was talking to Hatfield's family at the wake, he realized that the note was in the pocket of the jacket he was wearing. He announced to the family, "Hat handed me a note just before he died. I haven't read it yet, but knowing him, I'm sure there's a word of inspiration for us all." And he read aloud, "'You're standing on my oxygen tube!'"

It's ironic that a philosophical movement that depends on precise use of language should have developed among the British, of all people, as a number of jokes poke fun at the fact that they are often quite flummoxed by language.

The rector of a parish in the Church of England is visited by one of his parishioners, who says, "Reverend, recently I heard an amusing limerick that you might like, but I must warn you, it's a bit off-color."

"Oh, quite all right," says the rector. "I don't mind a bit of ribaldry now and then."

"Okay, here goes:

> *There once was a young man named Skinner,*
> *Who had a young lady to dinner.*
> *They sat down to dine*
> *At a quarter to nine,*
> *And by 9:45, it was in her.*

"What was in her," asks the rector. "The dinner?"

"No, Reverend, it was Skinner. Skinner was in her."

"Oh, good grief, yes. Quite! Very amusing."

A few weeks later, the rector is visited by his bishop, and he says, "Bishop, one of my parishioners told me an amusing limerick that I would like very much to tell you, if you don't mind its being a bit lewd."

"Please do," says the bishop.

"It goes like this," says the rector:

> *There once was a young man named Tupper,*
> *Who had a young lady to supper.*
> *First they had tea*
> *At a quarter to three,*
> *And by 3:45, it was up her.*

"Up her?" says the bishop. "What was up her? The supper?"

"No, no, Bishop. Actually, it was a complete stranger named Skinner."

These are the people who gave us ordinary language philosophy?

The Linguistic Status of Proper Names

For the past fifty years or so philosophy has become increasingly technical, less concerned with broadly framed questions like free will or the existence of God, and more finely focused on questions of logical and linguistic clarity. We're not naming names, but some of these philosophers seem to have gone off the deep end, like recent philosophers who have become intrigued by what sort of meaning proper names have. Bertrand Russell's view was that names are really abbreviated descriptions. "Michael Jackson," for example, is simply shorthand for "pink-skinned singer with unusual nose job."

For the contemporary philosopher who goes by the name "Saul Kripke," names of individuals have no descriptive definitions at all. They are "rigid designators," (or in ordinary English, labels); their only connection to the persons or things they name is the historical chain of transmission through which they have been passed down.

When he went into show business, Myron Feldstein changed his name to Frank Williamson. To celebrate landing a starring role on Broadway, he gave a huge party in his penthouse condo. He invited his mother to the party, but she never arrived.

The next morning he found his mother sitting in the lobby. He asked her what she was doing there, and why she hadn't come to the party.

"I couldn't find your apartment," she said.

"Well, why didn't you ask the doorman?"

"Believe me, I thought of that. But to tell you the truth, I forgot your name."

Frank, or as his mother would have it, Myron, has interrupted the historical chain of transmission of "Myron."

QUIZ

Whose theory of names, Russell's or Kripke's, is at play in the following joke?

A young man was shipwrecked alone on a desert island. One day, he saw a swimmer coming toward him. It was none other than Halle Berry! In a matter of hours, the two became passionate lovers. Weeks of fiery lovemaking followed. Then one day the man said to Halle, "Will you do me a special favor?"

"Anything," the beautiful woman replied.

"Great. Would you cut your hair very short and let me call you Ted?"

"Ooh, that sounds kind of weird," said Halle.

"Just do it—please, please, please?"

"Well, okay," said Halle.

That evening, as they strolled hand-in-hand along the shore, the young man turned to her and said, "Ted, you'll never believe who I'm shagging!"

The Philosophy of Fuzziness

One contemporary, technical, linguistic concept goes by the deceptively banal name of "vagueness." "Vagueness" is a term used by philosophers called "fuzzy logicians" (honest to God) to describe the quality of "having a truth-value of one to ten" rather than being simply and absolutely true or false. "That man is bald," for example, might be used to refer to anyone from Michael Jordan to Woody Harrelson. From Woody's point of view, the term is way too vague.

Some philosophers have seen vagueness as a pervasive defect of natural languages—say, Swedish or Swahili—and have advocated the construction of an artificial language, like mathematics, to eliminate vagueness.

In the following story, the guard is trying to mix a vague natural language and a precise mathematical language with predictable results:

Some tourists at the Museum of Natural History are marvelling at the dinosaur bones. One of them asks the guard, "Can you tell me how old these bones are?"

The guard replies, "They're three million, four years and six months old."

"That's an awfully exact number," says the tourist. "How do you know their age so precisely?"

The guard answers, "Well, the dinosaur bones were three million years old when I started working here, and that was four and a half years ago."

William James described a spectrum of ways of thinking, ranging from "tender-minded" to "tough-minded." More tender-minded philosophers maintain that vague, natural languages have an advantage over mathematics: They give us more wiggle room.

An eighty-year-old woman bursts into the men's day-room at the retirement home. She holds her clenched fist in the air and announces, "Anyone who can guess what I have in my hand can have sex with me tonight!"

An old man in the back shouts, "An elephant?"

The woman thinks for a moment and says, "Close enough!"

Tough-minded philosophers might grant this woman some wiggle room, but they would point to instances where precision is important and the vagueness of natural languages could be disastrous. Perhaps an artificial language could have averted the following tragedy:

An emergency medical dispatcher receives a panicky call from a hunter. "I've just come across a bloodstained body in the woods! It's a man, and I think he's dead! What should I do?"

The dispatcher calmly replies, "It's going to be all right, sir. Just follow my instructions. The first thing is to put the phone down and make sure he's dead."

There's a silence on the phone, followed by the sound of a shot. The man's voice returns, "Okay. Now what do I do?"

Vagueness Rules!

True story:

Guy Goma was sitting in a reception room at the BBC, waiting for a job interview for the position of data support person, when a television producer entered the room and asked, "Are you Guy Kewney?"

Mr. Goma, who is from the Congo and is a newcomer to the English language, replied, "Yes."

The producer whisked him into a studio, where the host of a live TV news programme was expecting to interview a business expert on the trademark dispute between Apple Computer and the Apple Corps recording company. "Were you surprised by the verdict today?" asked the interviewer.

After a moment of sheer panic, Mr. Goma decided to give it his best shot. "I am very surprised to see this verdict, because I was not expecting that," he answered.

"A big surprise," said his host.

"Exactly," replied Mr. Goma.

The interviewer asked if the verdict would allow more people to download music, and Mr. Goma allowed that more and more people will be downloading music in the future.

The interviewer concurred. "Thanks very much indeed!" he exclaimed.

DIMITRI: This clarifies everything we've been talking about.

TASSO: In what way?

DIMITRI: What you call "philosophy," I call "a joke."

Social and Political Philosophy

Social and political philosophy examines issues of justice in society. Why do we need governments? How should goods be distributed? How can we establish a fair social system? These questions used to be settled by the stronger guy hitting the weaker guy over the head with a bone, but after centuries of social and political philosophy, society has come to see that missiles are much more effective.

DIMITRI: Tasso, we can talk philosophy until we're blue in the face, but when push comes to shove, all I really want from life is my own little house, a sheep, and three square meals a day.

Tasso shoves Dimitri.

DIMITRI: What was that about?

TASSO: What's to stop me from shoving you—or anybody else—when I feel like it?

DIMITRI: The Guardians of the State, that's who!

TASSO: But how do they know what to do or why?

DIMITRI: By Zeus, we're talking philosophy again, aren't we?

The State of Nature

Political philosophers in the seventeenth and eighteenth centuries, such as Thomas Hobbes, John Locke, and Jean-Jacques Rousseau, traced the impetus for forming a government to man's insecurity in living in the rough-and-tumble of the state of nature. These philosophers weren't just talking about the perils of wild beasts in nature; they were talking about lawlessness: the risks of two-way traffic, noisy neighbours, wife-stealing, that sort of thing. These inconveniences led men and women to organize themselves into sovereign states. Limits on individual freedoms were accepted as fair exchange for the benefits of the state.

A wild rabbit was caught and taken to a National Institutes of Health laboratory. When he arrived, he was befriended by a rabbit that had been born and raised in the lab.

One evening the wild rabbit noticed that his cage hadn't been properly closed and decided to make a break for freedom. He invited the lab rabbit to join him. The lab rabbit was unsure, as he had never been outside the lab, but the wild rabbit finally convinced him to give it a try.

Once they were free, the wild rabbit said, "I'll show you the number-three best field," and took the lab rabbit to a field full of lettuce.

After they had eaten their fill, the wild rabbit said, "Now I'll show you the number-two best field," and took the lab rabbit to a field full of carrots.

After they had had their fill of carrots, the wild rabbit said, "Now I'll show you the number-one best field," and took the lab rabbit to a warren full of female bunnies. It was Heaven— nonstop lovemaking all night long.

As dawn was beginning to break, the lab rabbit announced that he would have to be getting back to the lab.

"Why?" said the wild rabbit. "I've shown you the number-three best field with the lettuce, the number-two best field with the carrots, and the number-one best field with the ladies. Why do you want to go back to the lab?"

The lab rabbit replied, "I can't help it. I'm dying for a cigarette!"

Such are the benefits of an organized society.

Describing what human life would be without government, Hobbes famously deemed man's natural state as, "solitary, poore [*sic*], nasty, brutish, and short." As far as we know, Hobbes was not much of a comic, but there is always something funny about lists that insert a clinker at the end, like the lady who complained that the food at her resort was "cold, undercooked, repulsive—and the portions were too small."

Might Equals Right

Niccolò Machiavelli, the sixteenth-century author of *The Prince*, is known as the father of modern statecraft because he advised Renaissance princes to disregard accepted standards of virtue and "enter into evil when necessitated." He recognized

no higher authority than the state, so his advice to princes was
. . . well, Machiavellian. He admitted right up front that his
criterion for virtue was whatever allowed the prince to survive
politically. While it is better for the prince to be feared than
loved, he should avoid being hated, as that could jeopardize his
power. Best of all is to mercilessly pursue power while appearing
upright. To wit:

A woman sues a man for defamation of character, charging
that he called her a pig. The man is found guilty and made to pay
damages. After the trial, he asks the judge, "Does this mean that I
can no longer call Ms. Harding a pig?"

The judge says, "That is correct."

"And does it mean that I can't call a pig Ms. Harding?"

"No," says the judge, "you are free to call a pig Ms. Harding.
There is no crime in that."

The man looks Ms. Harding in the eye and says, "Good
afternoon, Ms. Harding."

Jokes have always recognized that Machiavellian deceit,
especially when we're pretty sure we won't get caught, tempts
us all.

A man wins $100,000 in Las Vegas and, not wanting anyone to
know about it, he takes it home and buries it in his backyard. The
next morning he goes out back and finds only an empty hole. He
sees footprints leading to the house next door, which belongs to a
deaf-mute, so he asks the professor down the street, who knows

sign language, to help him confront his neighbour. The man takes his pistol, and he and the professor knock on the neighbour's door. When the neighbour answers, the man waves the pistol at him and says to the professor, "You tell this guy that if he doesn't give me back my $100,000, I'm going to kill him right now!"

The professor conveys the message to the neighbour, who responds that he hid the money in his own backyard under the cherry tree.

The professor turns to the man and says, "He refuses to tell you. He says he'd rather die first."

Unsurprisingly, Machiavelli was a proponent of the death penalty, because it was in the best interest of the prince to be seen as severe rather than merciful. In other words, he agreed with the cynic who said, "Capital punishment means never having to say, 'You again?'"

No matter how upright we may appear on the surface—or even in our own minds—Machiavelli believed that we're all Machiavellian at heart.

Mrs. Parker is called to serve on an American jury but asks to be excused because she doesn't believe in capital punishment. The public defender says, "But, madam, this isn't a murder trial. It's a civil suit. A woman is suing her former husband because he gambled away the $25,000 he promised to spend to remodel the bathroom for her birthday."

"Okay, I'll serve," says Mrs. Parker. "I suppose I could be wrong about capital punishment."

But wait one second. Could it be that the joke's on us? Some historians now believe Machiavelli was pulling our leg with a kind of reverse Machiavellianism—appearing evil while actually subscribing to old-time virtues. In the end, was Machiavelli actually satirizing despotism? In his essay "The Prince: Political Science or Political Satire?" Pulitzer Prize–winning historian Garrett Mattingly argues that Machiavelli has gotten a bum rap: "The notion that this little book [*The Prince*] was meant as a serious, scientific treatise on government contradicts everything we know about Machiavelli's life, about his writings, and about the history of his time."

In other words, Mattingly thinks Machiavelli was a sheep in wolf's clothing

---

Feminism

Here is a riddle that has baffled people for decades:

A man witnesses his son in a terrible bicycle accident. He scoops up his boy, puts him in the back of his car, and races to the emergency room. As the boy is rolled into surgery, the surgeon says, "Oh, my God! It's my son!"
How is this possible?

Du-*uh*! The surgeon is his mother.

Today, not even Nigel Farage would be puzzled by this riddle; the number of female M.D.s in this country is rapidly approaching the number of male M.Ds. And that is a result of the power of late-twentieth-century feminist philosophy.

When the BBC ran a listener poll for the world's greatest philosopher, nary a woman philosopher made the cut of the top twenty. (Karl Marx won.) Women scholars around the world were infuriated. Where was the neo-Platonist Greek philosopher Hypatia? Or the medieval essayist Hildegard of Bingen? Why is the twelfth century's Heloise excluded, while Abelard, who learned as much from her as she did from him, racks up votes (although he didn't make the top twenty either)? How about the seventeenth century's Mary Astell, a proto-feminist? And where are the modern era's Hannah Arendt, Iris Murdoch, and Ayn Rand?

Is academia hopelessly chauvinistic, resulting in the educated public's ignorance of these great philosophers? Or were the pigs of their day to blame for not taking these women seriously enough at the time?

The real dawn of feminist philosophy dates to the eighteenth century and Mary Wollstonecraft's seminal (or should we say ovarian?) work, *A Vindication of the Rights of Women*.

In that treatise, she takes on none other than Jean-Jacques Rousseau for proposing an inferior education system for women.

Feminism got an existentialist reinterpretation in the twentieth century with the publication of *The Second Sex* by philosopher (and paramour of Jean-Paul Sartre) Simone de Beauvoir. She declared that there is no such thing as essential womanhood, which she thought was a straitjacket imposed on women by men. Rather, women are free to create their own version of what it is to be a woman.

But how elastic is the concept of womanhood? Does the reproductive equipment we are born with have nothing to do with our gender identity? Some post-de Beauvoir feminists think so. They claim we are all born a blank slate sexually; our gender identity is something we gain later from society and our parents. And these days learning gender roles has become trickier than ever.

Two gay men are standing on a street corner when a gorgeous and shapely blonde strolls by in a low-cut, clingy chiffon dress.
Says one of the men to the other, "At times like this, I wish I were a lesbian!"

Are traditional gender roles a mere social construct, invented by men to keep women subservient? Or are those roles biologically determined? This enigma continues to divide philosophers and psychologists alike. Some deep thinkers land firmly on the side of biologically determined differences. For example, when Freud declared that "anatomy is destiny," he was employing a teleological argument to make the case that the way the female body is constructed determines women's role in society. It is unclear what anatomical attributes he was referring to when he concluded that women should do the ironing. There's also the question of whether men are biologically determined too. For example, as a result of their anatomy are men predisposed to use primitive criteria in choosing a spouse?

A man is dating three women and is trying to decide which to marry. He gives each of them £5,000 to see what they do with the money.

The first has a total makeover. She goes to a fancy salon, gets her hair, nails, and face done, and buys several new outfits. She tells him she has done this to be more attractive to him because she loves him so much.

The second buys the man a number of gifts. She gets him a new set of golf clubs, some accessories for his computer, and some expensive clothes. She tells him that she has spent all the money on him because she loves him so much.

The third woman invests the money in the stock market. She earns several times the £5,000. She gives him back his £5,000 and reinvests the remainder in a joint account. She tells him she wants to invest in their future because she loves him so much.

Which one does he choose?

Answer: the one with the biggest boobs.

QUIZ

Is this an anti-feminist joke or an anti-chauvinist-pig joke? Discuss.

Here's another text that argues for an essential difference between men and women. It's got to be essential because the First Man was free of social constructs and his impulsiveness was therefore innate.

God appears to Adam and Eve in the Garden and announces that he has two gifts, one for each of them, and he would like them to decide who gets which gift. He says, "The first gift is the ability to pee standing up."

Impulsively, Adam yells out, "Pee standing up? Hot dog! That sounds really cool! I want that one."

"Okay," says God, "that one's yours, Adam. Eve, you get the other one—multiple orgasms."

The social and political results of feminism are legion: voting rights, rape-victim-protection laws, better treatment and compensation in the workplace. Recently, another social fallout of feminism has been male backlash. From this a new category has arisen: the politically incorrect joke.

Calling any joke that pokes fun at feminism politically incorrect adds a new dimension to the joke—"I know this joke goes against accepted liberal philosophy, but hey, can't you have fun anymore?" By bracketing a joke in this way, the joker makes a claim for irreverence, a quality that can make a joke even funnier, and more socially perilous to the joker, as seen in this over-the-top joke:

On a transatlantic flight, a plane passes through a severe storm. The turbulence is awful, and things go from bad to worse when one wing is struck by lightning.

One woman in particular loses it. She stands up in the front of the plane screaming, "I'm too young to die!" Then she yells, "Well, if I'm going to die, I want my last minutes on earth to be memorable! No one has ever made me really feel like a woman! Well, I've had it! Is there *anyone* on this plane who can make me feel like a *woman*?"

For a moment there is silence. Everyone has forgotten his own peril, and they all stare, riveted, at the desperate woman in the front of the plane. Then a man stands up in the rear. He's a tall, tanned hunk with jet-black hair, and he starts to walk slowly up the aisle, unbuttoning his shirt. "I can make you feel like a woman," he says.

No one moves. As the man approaches, the woman begins to get excited. He removes his shirt. Muscles ripple across his chest as he reaches her, extends the arm holding his shirt to the trembling woman, and says, "Iron this."

In response to the onslaught of politically incorrect jokes came another new breed—stories that start out like the typical, chauvinist jokes of yore, but with an added twist in which the woman prevails.

Two bored male casino dealers are waiting at the craps table. A very attractive blonde woman arrives and bets £20,000 on a single roll of the dice. She says, "I hope you don't mind, but I feel much luckier when I'm completely nude." With that, she strips down, rolls the dice, and yells, "Come on, baby, Mama needs new clothes!" As the dice come to a stop she jumps up and down and squeals, "YES! YES! I WON, I WON!" She hugs each of the dealers, picks up her winnings and her clothes, and quickly departs. The dealers stare at each other dumbfounded. Finally, one of them asks, "What did she roll?" The other answers, "I don't know—I thought you were watching."

The moral: Not all blondes are dumb, but all men are men.

Here's another example from this neofeminist genre:

A blonde is sitting next to a lawyer on an aeroplane. The lawyer keeps bugging her to play a game with him by which they will see who has more general knowledge. Finally, he says he will offer her ten-to-one odds. Every time she doesn't know the answer to one of his questions, she will pay him five pounds. Every time he doesn't know the answer to one of her questions, he will pay her fifty pounds.

She agrees to play, and he asks her, "What is the distance from the earth to the nearest star?"

She says nothing, just hands him a five pound note.

She asks him, "What goes up a hill with three legs and comes back down with four legs?"

He thinks for a long time but in the end has to concede that he has no idea. He hands her fifty pounds.

The blonde puts the money in her purse without comment.

The lawyer says, "Wait a minute. What's the answer to your question?"

Without a word she hands him five pounds.

Economic Philosophies

In the first sentence of Robert Heilbroner's classic book about economic theoreticians, *The Worldly Philosophers,* the author admits that "this is a book about a few men with a curious claim to fame." Yes, even economics has its own philosophers.

Scottish economics philosopher Adam Smith wrote his ovarian (or should we say seminal?) work *An Inquiry into the Nature and Causes of the Wealth of Nations* in the same year that America declared its independence. This work established the blueprint for free-market capitalism.

One of the strengths of capitalism, according to Smith, is that it promotes economic creativity. It seems that self-interest, like the prospect of a hanging, concentrates the mind.

A man walks into a bank and says he wants to borrow £200 for six months. The bank manager asks him what kind of collateral he has. The man says, "I have a Rolls Royce. Here are the keys. Keep it until the loan is paid off."

Six months later the man returns to the bank, repays the £200 plus £10 interest and takes back his Rolls. The loan officer says, "Sir, if I may ask, why would a man who drives a Rolls Royce need to borrow £200?"

The man replies, "I had to go to France for six months, and where else could I store a Rolls that long for £10?"

In capitalist theory, the "discipline of the market" regulates the economy. Good inventory control, for example, can provide a competitive advantage to a business.

Interviewer: Sir, you have amassed a considerable fortune over your lifetime. How did you make your money?

Millionaire: I made it all in the carrier pigeon business.

Interviewer: Carrier pigeons! That's fascinating! How many did you sell?

Millionaire: I only sold one, but he kept coming back.

As capitalism has evolved, economic philosophy has had to play catch-up. Innovations in the marketplace have introduced complexities not imagined by Adam Smith and the classical economics philosophers. Health insurance, for example, has created a context in which it is in the buyer's best interest to not get his money's worth. Buying pork-belly futures is clearly a different animal, so to speak, than buying a hog. One such innovation, in which the classical laws of the marketplace do not quite seem to apply, is the raffle.

Jean Paul, a Cajun, moved to Texas and bought a donkey from an old farmer for $100. The farmer agreed to deliver the donkey the next day.

The next day the farmer drove up and said, "Sorry, but I got some bad news. The donkey died."

"Well then, just give me my money back."

"Can't do that. I went and spent it already."

"OK then, just unload the donkey."

"What are you gonna do with him?"

"I'm gonna raffle him off."

"You can't raffle off a dead donkey!"

"Sure, I can. Watch me. I just won't tell anyone he's dead."

A month later the farmer met up with the Cajun and asked, "What happened with the dead donkey?"

"I raffled him off. I sold 500 tickets at $2 apiece and made a profit of $898."

"Didn't anyone complain?"

"Just the guy who won. So I gave him his $2 back."

The classical economists also didn't pay much attention to what we now call "hidden value"—for example, the uncompensated labour provided by stay-at-home mothers. This story illustrates the concept of hidden value:

A famous art collector is walking through the city when he notices a mangy cat lapping milk from a saucer in the doorway of a shop. He does a double-take. He knows that the saucer is extremely old and very valuable, so he walks casually into the shop and offers to buy the cat for two pounds.

The shopkeeper replies, "I'm sorry, but the cat isn't for sale."

The collector says, "Please, I need a hungry cat around the house to catch mice. I'll pay you twenty pounds for that cat."

The owner says, "Sold," and hands over the cat.

The collector continues, "Hey, for the twenty pounds I wonder if you could throw in that old saucer. The cat's used to it and it'll save me from having to get a dish."

The owner says, "Sorry, buddy, but that's my lucky saucer. So far this week I've sold thirty-eight cats."

To his credit, Adam Smith foresaw some of the pitfalls in un-restrained capitalism, like the growth of monopolies. But it took Karl Marx in the nineteenth century to construct an economics philosophy that attacked the inevitable unequal distribution of goods inherent in the very structure of capitalism. Come the revolution, the government of the common man, Marx said, will eliminate the disparity between rich and poor—a disparity that touches everything from ownership to credit.

We were down in Cuba to buy some embargoed cigars a while back when we stopped in a Havana comedy club and heard this routine:

José: What a crazy world! The rich, who could pay cash, buy on credit. The poor, who have no money, must pay cash. Wouldn't Marx say it should be the other way around? The poor should be allowed to buy on credit, and the rich should pay cash.

Manuel: But the shopkeepers who gave credit to the poor would soon become poor themselves!
José: All the better! Then they could buy on credit too!

According to Marx, the dictatorship of the common man that follows the revolution is itself followed by the "withering away of the state." Still, we think Karl Marx has gotten a bad rap as a radical anarchist.

QUIZ

Which of the Marxes is more of an anarchist? Karl, who said, "It is inevitable that the oppressed classes will rise up and throw off their chains." Or Groucho, who said, "Outside of a dog, a book is man's best friend. Inside a dog, it's too dark to read."

Perhaps you're asking yourself, "What exactly is the difference between capitalism and communism?" Perhaps not. In any case, it's really quite simple. Under capitalism, man exploits his fellow man. Under communism, the opposite is true.

This conundrum led to the compromise between capitalism and socialism known as social democracy, where benefits are provided for people unable to work and laws protect collective bargaining. But the compromise forced some lefties to make strange bedfellows.

A union man is at a convention in Paris and decides to visit a
brothel. He asks the madam, "Is this a union house?"

"No, it's not," she replies.

"So how much do the girls earn?" the union man asks.

"You pay me £100, the house gets £80 and the girl gets £20."

"That's crass exploitation!" the man says and stomps out.

Eventually, he finds a brothel where the madam says it's a union
house. "If I pay you £100, how much does the girl get?" he asks.

"She gets £80."

"That's great!" he says. "I'd like Collette."

"I'm sure you would," says the madam, "but Thérèse here has
seniority."

Economics theory is especially prone to the fallacy of
"drawing a distinction where there is no difference." For example, is there actually a difference in principle between
welfare for the poor and tax cuts for the rich?

In this joke, Mr. Fenwood is employing a strategy that
makes an economic distinction without a difference:

Mr. Fenwood had a cow but no place to pasture her. So he
went to see his neighbour, Mr. Potter, and offered to pay Potter
twenty pounds a month to keep the cow in Potter's pasture.
Potter agreed. Several months went by. The cow was pastured
at Mr. Potter's, but Mr. Fenwood had never given Mr. Potter any
money. Finally, Mr. Potter went to see Mr. Fenwood and said, "I
know you've been struggling financially, so how about if we strike
a deal? I've had your cow now for ten months,
so you owe me £200. I figure that's about what the cow is

worth. How about if I just keep the cow and we'll call it square?"

Fenwood thought for a minute and said, "Keep her one more month and you've got a deal!"

Philosophy of Law

The philosophy of law, or jurisprudence, studies basic questions like "What is the purpose of laws?"

There are several basic theories. "Virtue jurisprudence," derived from Aristotle's ethics, is the view that laws should promote the development of virtuous character. Proponents of virtue jurisprudence might argue that the purpose of the Public Decency Law (no peeing in the public square) is to promote the development of higher moral standards in all groups, especially public pee-ers. (However, a jury of his pee-ers might disagree.)

Deontology is the view, held by Immanuel Kant, that the purpose of laws is to codify moral duties. For the deontologists, the Anti-Peeing Law supports the duty of all citizens to respect the sensibilities of others.

The nineteenth-century utilitarian Jeremy Bentham said the purpose of laws is to produce the best consequences for the greatest number of people. The utilitarians might argue that the A.P.L. produces more good consequences for more people (the townsfolk), than it does negative consequences for the few public piddlers, who will have to change their long-standing social habits.

But as is usual in philosophy, the first question posed to these theorists by regular folks might be, "Is there any practical difference among your cute theories?" Any of the three theories could be used to justify not only the Public Decency Law, but also many well-established legal principles, such as the notion that imposing a penalty for a crime returns the scales of justice to equilibrium. You could justify punishment from a virtue development perspective (rehabilitation), a deontological perspective (penalizing violations of civic duty), or a utilitarian perspective (deterring future bad consequences).

Nonphilosophers might ask, "If you all agree on the outcome, what difference does it make *why* we impose penalties?" The only down-to-earth issue is how to establish a match between an illegal act—say, insulting an officer of the court—and a penalty—say, a fifty pound fine. How's this for a match?

A man waits all day in court for his traffic case to be heard. At long last it's his turn to stand before the judge, but the judge only tells him that he will have to come back tomorrow, as court is being adjourned for the day. In exasperation, the man snaps, "What the hell for?"

The judge snaps back, "Fifty pounds for contempt of court!"

The man pulls out his wallet. The judge says, "You don't have to pay today."

The man says, "I'm just checking to see if I have enough for two more words."

Another well-known legal principle is the unreliability of circumstantial evidence. Again, all three of the abstract theorists could support it. A theorist of virtue jurisprudence might argue that a high standard of fairness in the courtroom provides a model of virtue for the citizenry. To the deontologist, circumstantial evidence might violate a universal duty to be scrupulously fair to others. To the utilitarian, the use of circumstantial evidence might bring about the undesirable consequence of imprisoning an innocent person.

Again, the more practical among us might ask, "Who the heck cares *why* we treat circumstantial evidence cautiously?" As a practical matter, we need only make the case for its unreliability, as the woman in the following story does. (Note her deft use of *reductio ad absurdum*.)

A couple goes on holiday to a fishing resort. While he's napping, she decides to take his boat out on the lake and read. While she's soaking up the sun, the local warden comes by in a boat, and says, "There's no fishing allowed here, madam. I'm going to have to arrest you."

The woman says, "But, I'm not fishing."

The warden says, "Madam, you have all the necessary equipment. I'm going to have to call you in."

The woman says, "If you do that, I'm going to have to charge you with rape."

"But I haven't even touched you," says the warden.

"I know," she says, "but you have all the necessary equipment."

But it turns out there *are* legal principles where it makes a great deal of difference which basic theory we adopt, as this story shows.

A judge calls the opposing lawyers into his chambers, and says, "The reason we're here is that both of you have given me a bribe." Both lawyers squirm in their seats. "You, Alan, have given me £15,000. Phil, you gave me £10,000."

The judge hands Alan a cheque for £5,000 and says, "Now you're even, and I'm going to decide this case solely on its merits."

If the purpose of prohibiting bribes is only to outlaw violations of the duty to deal equitably with all, we might agree with the judge that taking equal bribes has the same result as taking no bribe. Ditto if the purpose of prohibiting bribes is to ensure even-handedness in the utilitarian production of good consequences. But it would be much more difficult to argue that taking equal bribes promotes virtue in either the judge or the attorneys.

Pretty neat how we got this far without telling a lawyer joke, right? But, hey, we're only human.

A Manhattan lawyer sends a note to a client:

"Dear Frank: I thought I saw you downtown yesterday. I crossed the street to say hello, but it wasn't you. One-tenth of an hour: $50."

DIMITRI: You've inspired me, Tasso. I've decided to run for Public Decency Officer. Can I count on your vote?

TASSO: Of course, my friend. As long as the election is by secret ballot.

Relativity

*What can we say? This term means different things
to different people.*

DIMITRI: The trouble with you, my friend, is you live too much
in your head.

TASSO: Compared to whom?

DIMITRI: Well, compared to Achilles, the athlete.

TASSO: How about compared to Socrates?

DIMITRI: Okay, you win again. Compared to Socrates, you're
a bozo.

Relative Truth

Is truth relative or absolute?

The ancient Taoist philosopher Chuang Tzu awoke from
a dream in which he was a butterfly, or, he wondered, was he
really a butterfly who was now dreaming he was Chuang Tzu?

In the modern Western world, philosophers have been obsessed by the relativity of knowledge to the knower. As we've seen, George Berkeley went so far as to say that "physical objects" only exist relative to the mind.

In the twentieth century, a Harvard professor experimented with psychedelic drugs and was fascinated by the relativity of his insights. When William James inhaled laughing gas, James thought he saw the ultimate unity of all things, but, after the drug wore off, he couldn't remember his cosmic insights. So, the story goes, the next time he sniffed laughing gas, he tied a pen to his hand and left his lab book open in front of him. Sure enough, a brilliant idea came to him, and this time he managed to get it down on paper. Hours later, in his unaltered state, he read the philosophical breakthrough he had recorded: "Everything has a petroleumlike smell!"

Disappointed at first, Professor James soon came to his philosophical senses. The real question, he realized, was whether a) ideas that appeared brilliant to him under the influence of laughing gas were actually banal; or b) the brilliance of "Everything has a petroleumlike smell" could not be properly appreciated unless one was under the influence of laughing gas.

There's something in James's analysis that has a certain jokelike smell.

Relativity of Time

Lots of jokes illustrate the relativity of the perception of time. For example:

A snail was mugged by two turtles. When the police asked him what happened, he said, "I don't know. It all happened so fast."

And here comes that snail again:

There's a knock on the door, but when the woman answers it, there's only a snail. She picks it up and throws it across the yard. Two weeks later, there's another knock on the door. The woman answers the door, and there's the snail again. The snail says, "What was that all about?"

The relativity between finite time and eternity has been a staple of philosophical thought, and so, naturally, a staple for jokesters.

A man is praying to God. "Lord," he prays, "I would like to ask you a question."

The Lord responds, "No problem. Go ahead."

"Lord, is it true that a million years to you is but a second?"

"Yes, that is true."

"Well, then, what is a million pounds to you?"

"A million pounds to me is but a penny."

"Ah, then, Lord," says the man, "may I have a penny?"

"Sure," says the Lord. "Just a second."

"*We won't publish your book,* The Life of a Mayfly:
an Autobiography, *because it's only a page long.*

Relativity of Worldviews

There is a whole shelf full of jokes that illustrate the relativity of different points of view.

> A Frenchman walks into a bar. There's a parrot wearing a tuxedo perched on his shoulder. The bartender says, "Wow, that's cute. Where did you get that?"
>
> The parrot says, "In France. They've got millions of guys like this over there."

The twentieth-century American philosopher W.V.O. Quine wrote that our worldview is relative to our native language, a framework we are unable to climb out of for a different perspective. We cannot know for certain how to translate a term in an unrelated language into our own language. We *can* see that the speaker of another language points to the same object when he says *"gavagai"* as the one we point to when we say "rabbit," but we cannot be sure whether he means "the fusion of rabbit parts" or "the succession of rabbit stages" or something else rabbitty.

> Two Jewish guys have dinner in a kosher Chinese restaurant. The Chinese waiter makes small talk with them in Yiddish as they look over the menu and then takes their order in Yiddish. On the way out, the men tell the Jewish owner what a pleasant surprise it was to be able to converse in Yiddish with the waiter.
>
> "Shh," says the owner. "He thinks he's learning English."

This provides a dead-on analogy to Quine's notion of the problem of radical translation. The Chinese waiter can relate all Yiddish words to each other in the same way as the Jewish diners. His *whole* knowledge of Yiddish however, is off track in one important, *systematic* way: He thinks it's English!

Even the very idea of what counts as a foreign language may be relative to the speaker. Consider the following story from the world of international commerce:

A multinational corporation advertises for a secretary. A golden retriever applies for the job, passes the typing test, and is granted an interview. The human-resources manager asks, "Do you speak any foreign languages?"

And the golden retriever says, "Meow."

Relativity of Values

In our own day, Michel Foucault focused on another kind of relativity—the relativity of cultural values to social power. Our cultural values, particularly what we count as normal, determine and are determined by how society exercises control. Who counts as mentally ill? Who gets to determine that? What does it mean to be designated mentally ill for those who are so designated? What does it mean for those who get to control them? And who *are* those who get to control them? The answers to these questions change over time as the power arrangements in society shift. In one age, the priests are the controlling group; in another, the doctors. This has implications for how the so-called mentally ill get treated. The bottom line is that the values we think are timeless and absolute are really in constant historical flux relative to who has power and how it gets used.

> Pat: Mike, I'm calling you from the motorway on my new phone.
> Mike: Be careful, Pat. They just said on the radio that there's a nut driving the wrong way on the motorway.
> Pat: One nut? Hell, there are hundreds of them!

From the standpoint of pure reason, Pat is just as right as the man on the radio. Relative to him, everyone else *is* going the wrong way. So why is the joke a joke instead of simply a clash of two points of view? Because of Foucault's point, which is that the state ultimately gets to decide what's the right way to go.

Another concern of philosophers since Plato has been the relativity between temporal values and eternal values. And once again a joke puts it in perspective:

> There once was a rich man who was near death. He was very much aggrieved because he had worked very hard for his money, and he wanted to be able to take it with him to Heaven. So he began to pray that he might be able to take some of his wealth.
> An angel heard his plea and appeared to him. "Sorry, but you can't take your wealth with you." The man implored the angel to speak to God to see if He might bend the rules.

The angel reappeared and announced that God had decided to make an exception and was allowing him to take one suitcase with him. Overjoyed, the man gathered his largest suitcase, filled it with pure gold bars, and placed it beside his bed.

Soon afterward the man died and showed up at the pearly gates. St. Peter, seeing the suitcase, said, "Hold on, you can't bring that in here!"

But the man explained to St. Peter that he had permission and asked him to verify his story with the Lord. Sure enough, St. Peter returned, saying, "You're right. You are allowed one carry-on bag, but I'm supposed to check its contents before letting it through."

St. Peter opened the suitcase to inspect the worldly items that the man found too precious to leave behind and exclaimed, "You brought pavement?"

Absolute Relativity

Much philosophical error stems from treating relative points of view as though they were absolute. Thomas Jefferson, borrowing from the British philosopher John Locke, found the right to life, liberty, and the pursuit of happiness to be "self-evident," presumably because he thought they were universal and absolute. But this is clearly not so self-evident to a person from another culture—say, a radical Islamist who thinks pursuing happiness is exactly what characterizes an infidel.

The opposite error is possible too. We may attribute relativity to something that is absolute.

The lookout on a battleship spies a light ahead off the starboard bow. The captain tells him to signal the other vessel, "Advise you change course twenty degrees immediately!"

The answer comes back, "Advise *you* change course twenty degrees immediately!"

The captain is furious. He signals, "I am a captain. We are on a collision course. Alter your course twenty degrees *now!*"

The answer comes back, "I am a seaman second class, and I strongly urge you to alter *your* course twenty degrees."

Now the captain is beside himself with rage. He signals, "I am a battleship!"

The answer comes back, "I am a lighthouse."

Keep in mind these deep thoughts on relativity the next time you send out for Chinese food—or, as the Chinese call it, food.

DIMITRI: So, Tasso, you seem to be one of those guys who thinks there is no absolute truth, that all truth is relative.

TASSO: Right.

DIMITRI: Are you sure of that?

TASSO: Absolutely.

Metaphilosophy

*The philosophy of philosophy. Not to be confused with the philosophy
of the philosophy of philosophy.*

DIMITRI: I'm really getting the hang of this now, Tasso.

TASSO: The hang of what?

DIMITRI: Philosophy, of course!

TASSO: You call this philosophy?

The prefix *meta*, which basically means "beyond and inclusive of
all below," pops up all over the place in philosophical discourse,
like in metalanguage, a language that can be used to describe
language. Or in metaethics, which investigates where our ethical
principles come from, and what they mean. So it was only a *meta*
of time before metaphilosophy appeared on the scene.

Metaphilosophy wrestles with that burning question, "What
is philosophy?" You'd think philosophers would have known
the answer to that one going in. It makes you wonder how they

knew they wanted to become philosophers in the first place. We never hear about hairdressers pondering the question, "What is hairdressing?" If a hairdresser doesn't know what hairdressing is by now, he's in the wrong line of work. We sure as hell wouldn't want him giving our wives an updo.

Nonetheless, modern philosophers are continually redefining philosophy. In the twentieth century, Rudolf Carnap and the logical positivists defined away a huge hunk of philosophy when they announced that metaphysics is meaningless. They said the sole task of philosophy is to analyze scientific sentences.

And Carnap's contemporary, Ludwig Wittgenstein, the godfather of ordinary language philosophy, went even further. He thought his first major book had brought the history of philosophy to a close, because he had demonstrated that all philosophical propositions were meaningless—*including his own*. He was so convinced that he had closed the book on philosophy that he settled down to teach primary school. A few years later he reopened the book of philosophy with a new conception of its purpose—therapy, of all things. By that, Ludwig meant that if we straighten out confusing language, we will cure ourselves of the blues brought on by nonsensical philosophical questions.

In our own day, "modal logicians"—logicians who differentiate between statements that are *possibly* true and those that are *necessarily* true—worry about which category their own statements fall into. It sounds to us like metastatements all the way down.

It is in this tradition of metaphilosophy that we find Seamus.

Seamus was about to go on his first date, so he asked his brother, the ladies' man, for advice. "Give me some tips on how to talk to them."

"Here's the secret," said his brother. "Irish girls like to talk about three things: food, family, and philosophy. If you ask a girl what she likes to eat, it shows you're interested in her. If you ask her about her family, it shows your intentions are honourable. If you discuss philosophy, it shows you respect her intelligence."

"Gee, thanks," said Seamus. "Food, family, philosophy. I can handle that."

That night as he met the young lady, Seamus blurted out, "Do you like cabbage?"

"Uh, no," said the puzzled girl.

"Do you have a brother?" asked Seamus.

"No."

"Well, *if* you had a brother, would he like cabbage?"

That's philosophy.

Contemporary philosopher William Vallicella writes, "Metaphilosophy is the philosophy of philosophy. It is itself a branch of philosophy, unlike the philosophy of science, which is not a branch of science, or the philosophy of religion, which is not a branch of religion."

It is statements like this that have made Vallicella such
a hot ticket on the party circuit.

The deep, underlying thesis of this book is right once again.
If there is metaphilosophy, there must be metajokes.

A travelling salesman was driving in the country when his car
broke down. He hiked several miles to a farmhouse, and asked
the farmer if there was a place he could stay overnight. "Sure,"
said the farmer, "my wife died several years ago, and my two
daughters are twenty-one and twenty-three, but they're off at
university, and I'm all by myself, so I have lots of room to put you
up."

Hearing this, the salesman turned around and started walking
back towards the road.

The farmer called after him, "Didn't you hear what I said?
I have lots of room."

"I heard you," said the salesman, "but I think I'm in the wrong
joke."

And, of course, the *ur*-metajoke:

A blind man, a Lesbian, and a frog walk into a bar. The barman
looks at them and says, "What is this—a joke?"

And finally, a politically incorrect metajoke. Just as metaphilosophy requires the metaphilosopher to have some
knowledge of what philosophy is generally understood to

be, metajokes require knowledge of what a joke is generally understood to be—in this case, an Irish joke.

A guy walks into a crowded bar and announces that he's got a terrific Irish joke to tell. But before he can start, the barman says, "Hold it right there, pal. I'm Irish."

And the guy says, "Okay, I'll tell it very, very slowly."

DIMITRI: So we've spent the whole afternoon discussing philosophy and you don't even know what philosophy is?

TASSO: Why do you ask?

Summa Time: A Conclusion

*A cogent and comprehensive review of
everything we have learned today*

Tasso takes the mike at the Acropolis Comedy Club.

TASSO: But seriously, folks . . . Did you hear about the British empiricist who told his wife she was nothing but a collection of sense data?

"Oh, yeah?" she said. "How do you think it feels going to bed every night with a man who's got no *ding an sich*?"

I'm not kidding, I was married for ten years before I realized that my wife was all existence and no essence. I mean her *esse* really *was percipi*.

What'sa matter, folks? It's so quiet in here, you could hear a tree fall in the forest . . . even if you *weren't* there! Schopenhauer said there would be nights like this.

Kids today, huh? The other day my son asked me for the keys to the car, and I said, "Son, in the best of all possible worlds you'd have your own car."

And he said, "But, Dad, this isn't the best of all possible worlds."

And I said, "So go live with your mother!"

By the way, a funny thing happened on my way over here tonight: I stepped in the same river . . . *twice!*

Hey, the other day Plato and a platypus walked into a bar. The bartender gave the philosopher a quizzical look, and Plato said, "What can I say? She looked better in the cave."

DIMITRI (from audience): Give him the hook!

GREAT MOMENTS IN
THE HISTORY OF PHILOSOPHY

530 B.C. On the eighty-third day under the bodhi-tree, Gautama smiles inscrutably at a knock-knock joke.

Gautama Buddha, 563–483 B.C.

Zeno of Elea, 490–425 B.C.
Socrates, 469–399 B.C.

381 B.C. Plato sees shadows on the wall of a cave and interprets them to mean six more weeks of winter.

399 B.C. Socrates has a hemlock and soda—with a twist.

Plato, 427–347 B.C.
Aristotle, 384–322 B.C.
Stoics, began in 4th century B.C.

399 A.D. A review in *Alexandria Asp* dismisses Hypatia's Neoplatonism as "chick lit."

St. Augustine, 354–430 a.d.
Hypatia, 370–415 A.D.

| **6TH CENTURY B.C.** | **5TH CENTURY B.C.** | **4TH CENTURY B.C.** | **4TH CENTURY A.D.** |

1328 William Occam invents the Gillette Mach 3.

William Occam, 1285–1347

1504 A prankster puts a "Random Acts of Kindness" bumper sticker on Nick Machiavelli's carriage.

Niccoló Machiavelli, 1469–1527

1650 René Descartes stops thinking for a second and dies.

1652 Pascal goes to Longchamp racetrack where he wagers a wad on a horse named Mon Dieu. He loses.

Thomas Hobbes, 1588–1679
René Descartes, 1596–1650
Blaise Pascal, 1623–1662
Baruch Spinoza, 1632–1677
John Locke, 1632–1704
Gottfried W. von Leibniz, 1646–1716

14TH CENTURY

16TH CENTURY

17TH CENTURY

1731 Bishop Berkeley spends thirty days in a sensory-deprivation tank and emerges with mind unchanged.

1754 Immanuel Kant has a direct encounter with a *ding an sich*—says he "can't talk about it."

1792 A review in *Manchester Guardian* dismisses Mary Wollstonecraft's *A Vindication of the Rights of Women* as "chick lit."

George Berkeley, 1685–1753
David Hume, 1711–1776
Jean-Jacques Rousseau, 1712–1778
Adam Smith, 1723–1790
Immanuel Kant, 1724–1804
Mary Wollstonecraft, 1759–1797

1818 Older brothers Chico, Groucho, Gummo, Harpo, and Zeppo welcome baby Karl into world.

1844 Tired of always being called the "Melancholy Dane," Kierkegaard attempts to change his citizenship

1900 Nietzsche dies; God dies six months later of a broken heart.

Jeremy Bentham, 1748–1832
G. W. F. Hegel, 1770–1831
Arthur Schopenhauer, 1788–1860
John Stuart Mill, 1806–1873
Søren Kierkegaard, 1813–1855
Karl Marx, 1818–1883
William James, 1842–1910
Friedrich Nietzsche, 1844–1900
Edmund Husserl, 1859–1938

18TH
CENTURY

19TH
CENTURY

1954 Jean-Paul Sartre abandons his philosophical career to become a waiter.

1958 A review in *Le Monde* dismisses Simone de Beauvoir's *The Second Sex* as *"littérature des chicks."*

1996 Moonlighting in the WWE, Kripke has his name officially changed to The Rigid Designator.

Alfred North Whitehead, 1861–1947
Bertrand Russell, 1872–1970
Ludwig Wittgenstein, 1889–1951
Martin Heidegger, 1889–1976
Rudolf Carnap, 1891–1970
Gilbert Ryle, 1900–1976
Karl Popper, 1902–1994
Jean-Paul Sartre, 1905–1980
Simone de Beauvoir, 1908–1986
W.V.O. Quine, 1908–2000
John Austin, 1911–1960
Albert Camus, 1913–1960
Michel Foucault, 1926–1984
Saul Kripke, 1940–
Peter Singer, 1946–

analytic statement: A statement that is true by definition. For example, "All ducks are birds" is analytic because part of what we mean by "duck" is that it is a member of the bird family. "All birds are ducks," on the other hand, is not analytic because duckiness is not part of the definition of "bird." Obviously, "All ducks are ducks," is analytic, as is "All birds are birds." It is heartening to see the practical help that philosophy can provide to other disciplines, such as ornithology. Contrast **synthetic statement**.

a posteriori: Known by experience; known **empirically**. In order to know that some beers taste good but are not filling, you would have to experience/chug at least one beer that tastes good and is not filling. Contrast *a priori*.

a priori: Known *prior* to experience. For example, one can know, prior to ever watching the show, that all *American Idol* contestants believe they are singers because *American Idol* is a singing contest for people who—for reasons best known to themselves—believe they are singers. Contrast *a posteriori*.

deductive logic: Reasoning from a set of premises to a conclusion that can be logically inferred from them. The most basic form of deductive logic is the *syllogism*, e.g., "All comedians are philosophers; Larry, Moe, and Curly are comedians; therefore, Larry, Moe, and Curly are philosophers." Contrast **inductive logic.**

deontological ethics: Ethics based on the theory that moral obligation rests on duty (from the Greek *deon*), quite apart from the practical consequences of actions. For example, a political leader who believes his highest duty is to protect the public from terrorist attacks might argue that in order to fulfill this duty he has to plant hidden microphones in everybody's bedrooms, regardless of the consequences for your sex life.

***ding an sich*:** Thing-in-itself, as opposed to the sensory representations of a thing. The idea here is that an object is more than simply the sum of its sense data (i.e., what it looks, sounds, tastes, smells, and feels like), and that there is some thing-in-itself behind all this sense data that is separate from the data. Some philosophers believe this notion belongs in the same category as unicorns and Santa Claus.

emotivism: The ethical philosophy that moral judgments are neither true nor false, but merely express our approval or disapproval of an action or of an individual who performs a particular action or set of actions. In this philosophy, the statement, "Saddam is an evildoer," simply means, "Saddam is not my cup of tea. I don't know; I've just never cared for the guy."

empiricism: The view that experience, particularly sensory experience, is the primary—or the sole—path to knowledge. "How do you *know* there are unicorns?" "Because I just saw one in the garden!" Now, that's what we call x-treme empiricism.

Contrast **rationalism**.

essentialism: The philosophy that objects have essences, or essential qualities, which can be distinguished from their non-essential, or accidental, qualities. For example, it is an essential quality of a married man that he has a wife (possibly a male wife.) But it is only an accidental quality of a married man that he wears a wedding ring. He could still be a married man without wearing one, although his wife might argue the point.

existentialism: A school of philosophy that seeks to describe the actual conditions of our individual human existence rather than abstract, universal human qualities. Sartre's definition was "the view that existence precedes essence," meaning that the primary fact about us is our existence; we create our own essence. This has profound implications for existentialist ethics, which exhorts us to always live "authentically," fully conscious of our mortality and undeluded about the choices we make—in short, the kind of preoccupations that are best explored over coffee and cigarettes in a Parisian café, as compared to, say, over a conveyor belt on a Detroit assembly line.

inductive logic: Reasoning from specific instances to a general conclusion that is broader than what can be logically inferred from the instances. For example, our observation that the sun rose today, yesterday, and all the days we know about before yesterday gives rise to the conclusion that the sun has always come up and will continue to come up every day, even though this cannot be logically inferred from the known instances. Note: This example will not work for our readers at the North Pole. Contrast **deductive logic**.

infinite regress argument: An argument that a purported explanation is unsatisfactory because it gives rise to the need for an infinite series of such "explanations." For example, to explain the existence of the world by positing a "maker" raises the question of how to explain the existence of the maker. If another maker is posited, the question becomes, "Who made *that* maker?" And so on, ad infinitum. Or ad nauseam, whichever comes first.

koan: In Zen Buddhism, a riddle designed to shock us into sudden enlightenment. "What is the sound of one hand clapping?" seems to do the trick; "What is the sound of two hands clapping?" does not. See also *satori*.

Law of Noncontradiction: Aristotle's logical principle that a thing cannot be both A and not-A at the same time in the same respect. It would be self-contradictory to say, "Your pants are on fire, and, what's more, your pants are not on fire." (Under the circumstances, Aristotle's Law notwithstanding, it couldn't hurt to hose yourself down.)

noumenal: Pertaining to things as they are in themselves, as opposed to how they appear to our senses. See *ding an sich* . . . but then again, you can't, can you? Contrast **phenomenal**.

ordinary language philosophy: A philosophical movement that seeks to understand philosophical concepts by examining ordinary linguistic usage. According to philosophers of this school, many questions that have befuddled deep thinkers for millennia are only befuddling because of the ambiguities and logical mistakes inherent in the questions themselves. This marked the end of the Age of Befuddlement.

paradox: a) A piece of reasoning using apparently sound logic and apparently true premises that nevertheless results in a contradiction; b) any two physicians.

phenomenal: Pertaining to our sensory experience of objects. "That is a red hat" refers to our sensory experience of an object that appears red and hatlike. The locution, "Wow! Your red hat is phenomenal!" on the other hand, may be a red herring. Contrast **noumenal.**

phenomenology: A method of inquiry that attempts to describe reality as it is perceived and understood by human consciousness, as opposed, for example, to scientific description. Phenomenology, for instance, describes the phenomenon of "lived time," or time as we experience it, as compared to "clock time." In the movie *Manhattan*, when Woody Allen says, "We hardly ever make love—only twice a week," he is expressing "lived time"; likewise when his screen wife declares, "He *always* wants to make love—like twice a week!"

post hoc ergo propter hoc: A logical fallacy, meaning literally, "after this, therefore because of this"; the fallacy that because A precedes B, it must therefore be the cause of B. The book *Freakonomics* points out loads of these fallacies, especially in the realm of parenting. A parent says, "My kid is smart because I played Mozart to him while he was *in utero*," while in fact there is no correlation between these two circumstances. Chances are the kid is smart because he had parents who had heard of Mozart (i.e., were educated and therefore probably smart).

pragmatism: a school of philosophy that stresses the link between theory and practice. A true theory, for example, is defined by William James as a useful theory, or one that spawns further knowledge. Some people find James's definition useful; others don't.

rationalism: The view that reason is the primary—or the sole—path to knowledge. It is often contrasted with **empiricism**, which is the view that sensory experience is the primary path to knowledge. Traditionally, rationalists have preferred reason because the senses are notoriously unreliable and knowledge based on them is therefore uncertain. They preferred the flat-out *certainty* of statements arrived at by reason, such as, "This is the best of all possible worlds." You had to be there . . .

satori: In Zen Buddhism, an experience of enlightenment in which we suddenly see the true nature of ourselves and the world. To quote the Red Hot Chili Peppers, "If you have to ask, you don't know."

supreme categorical imperative: Immanuel Kant's overriding moral principle that one ought to act only according to those maxims that can be consistently willed as a universal law. It's sort of like the golden rule with umlauts, but not quite.

synthetic statement: A statement that is not true by definition. For example, "Yo mama wears army boots" is a synthetic statement; it adds information not included in the definition of the term "Yo mama." This is also true of the corollary "Yo Yo Ma wears army boots." Contrast **analytic statement**.

telos: Inner aim. The *telos* of an acorn is to become an oak tree. Similarly, the *telos* of a graduate student in philosophy is a tenured professorship at Harvard. This is his or her inner aim, despite the higher odds of a career at Wal-Mart.

utilitarianism: the moral philosophy that right actions are those that bring about more good for the persons affected than any alternative. The limited utility of this moral philosophy becomes evident when you try to please both your mother and your mother-in-law on Christmas Day.

ACKNOWLEDGMENTS

We don't know anybody other than ourselves who is willing to take responsibility for the idea for this book, but we do want to acknowledge a couple of joke-meisters who supplied us with some of our best gags: Gil Eisner and Herb Klein.

Professor Robert Wolff, our philosophy tutor at Harvard, deserves credit for teaching us to think philosophically . . . sort of.

Bill Hughes and Stefan Billups, photographers extraordinaire, made us look both smarter and funnier than we really are.

Thanks to Martha Harrington and Satch Lampron, innkeepers of the Nestle Inn in Conway, Massachusetts, our tolerant hosts during our marathon final edit.

No respectable acknowledgments page would be complete without a heartfelt smooch in the direction of our wives and daughters. You know who you are. And if not, those smooches are for Eloise and Freke, Esther and Samara (whose help went far beyond the bounds of filial duty).

We especially want to thank Julia Lord of Julia Lord Literary Management, our agent and a woman of astonishing intelligence and wit, not to mention patience.

Also, a tip of our collective hat to our editor, Ann Treistman, who steadily encouraged us to improve this manuscript in spite of ourselves.

David Rosen, vice president and publisher of Abrams Image, championed the book from the outset and became the head cheerleader for Team Plato. Thank you very much, David.

Finally, we want to express our belated apologies to Immanuel Kant for never completely understanding him. We feel your pain, Manny.

—TWC/DMK